Charles Haddon Spurgeon is on
who has been researched, stud.
extent that one has to query, 'Can anything else be written about
this man?' Yet, in this present new work – *The Child is Father of
the Man* – Tom Nettles has well proven there is still more to say
and consider about C. H. Spurgeon. While not writing a full-scale
biography, Nettles' approach brings in bold relief ten different issues
in the life and thought of Spurgeon which he advocates 'appeared
early in Spurgeon's life, made their way in his ministry through
the years, and stayed with him until his death.' The result of such a
study gives us what is perhaps the most, well-rounded treatment of
Charles Spurgeon that has been achieved in Spurgeonic literature.
Here we see what mattered above all things in Spurgeon's convictions
as a Christian, a churchman, a preacher, and a pastor-theologian.
However, the beauty in how Nettles unpacks this leaves the reader
not with Spurgeon's greatness but the greatness of the God and
Christ Spurgeon loved and labored to leave his own generation with,
which marked his faith as worthy to follow. Needless to say, Tom
Nettles has given the church a great gift in *The Child is Father of
the Man!* A must read not only for pastors but for all Christians
in learning how to love and serve Christ with unflinching fidelity.

KURT M. SMITH
Pastor, Providence Reformed Baptist Church, Remlap, Alabama, USA
Author of *Thundering the Word: The Awakening Ministry of George Whitefield*

After C. H. Spurgeon died in 1892, biographies streamed from the
presses at the incredible rate of one per month for the next two years.
Even the author of this volume, Tom Nettles, has already made a
masterful 900-page contribution to the massive library of Spurgeon
biographies. Why another? Though I could provide a number of
reasons, one is that God blessed C. H. Spurgeon with an influence
so vast that biographies tend to be written about the 'different'
Spurgeons: the preacher, the pastor, the writer, the evangelist, the
theologian, the sufferer, the educator, etc. The unique perspective
of this biography is perfectly summarized in the title: *The Child is*

Father of the Man. In this work Nettles shows how the remarkable fruitfulness of Spurgeon's ministry developed from tiny seeds sown in his childhood and youth. Readers will enjoy the remarkable insights from a writer who is not only a Spurgeon scholar, but a man who has served the church as a professor of historical theology for more than forty years.

DONALD S. WHITNEY

Professor of Biblical Spirituality and Associate Dean,
The Southern Baptist Theological Seminary, Louisville, Kentucky

Author of *Spiritual Disciplines for the Christian Life,
Praying the Bible,* and *Family Worship*

This is a sweet study of the character and labour of Spurgeon, ten bright themes woven into a compelling tapestry, bringing the man and his ministry into clear focus. There is depth in the study, and there is breadth, and – perhaps most preciously – there is a happy recognition of the grace of God, the beauty of Christ, and the power of the Spirit, upon which Spurgeon's ministry depended and in which he himself delighted. This is a book to instruct and encourage not only those who appreciate Spurgeon, but all who seek to serve his God and ours.

JEREMY WALKER

Pastor, Maidenbower Baptist Church, Crawley, UK

One of our era's most trusted and faithful church historians brings to life one of church history's most trusted and faithful preacher. Dr. Tom Nettles brilliantly focusses on ten key moments, convictions really, that shaped the larger-than-life Charles Haddon Spurgeon. These convictions steeled Spurgeon to weather controversy, depression, and setbacks. Through it all, Spurgeon's exuberant love for God, the gospel, and for the church shines through. This book will put wind in your sails.

STEPHEN J. NICHOLS

President, Reformation Bible College
Chief Academic Officer, Ligonier Ministries

This splendid volume on Charles Spurgeon is many things: it is packed with biography, history, and theology. But above all, it is a spiritual manual covering the major facets of the Christian life as Spurgeon experienced them: devotional Calvinism, conversionism, evangelistic fervor, sanctification through depression, severe opposition and controversy, and the Christian's relationship with Scripture. A must-read for Christian pilgrims on the way, especially for those needing encouragement in their walk with the Lord!

ROBERT W. CALDWELL
Professor of Church History, Southwestern Baptist Theological Seminary,
Forth Worth, Texas

Even for those who know Spurgeon well, this book offers fascinating insights, and a treasure trove of quotes from the 'prince of preachers'. Clustered around the convictions that drove Spurgeon, Tom Nettles produces almost a compendium of evangelical (Calvinist) theology, and does not hide from the controversies that followed Spurgeon's captivating life and ministry. Indeed the chapter on controversy, and 'the need for it', is worth the price of the book. You don't have to love Spurgeon, or Calvinism, or Baptist theology to profit from this book. But if, like me, you love all three (especially a Calvinism that is passionate about the lost), you will find it an absolute treat, and a robust foundation for your soul.

JEREMY MCQUOID
Teaching Pastor, Deeside Christian Fellowship, Aberdeen, Scotland
and Chair of Council, Keswick Ministries

The CHILD is FATHER of the MAN

Tom Nettles

CHRISTIAN
FOCUS

Scripture quotations are from *The Holy Bible, English Standard Version*, copyright © 2001 by Crossway Bibles, a publishing ministry of Good News Publishers. Used by permission. All rights reserved. ESV Text Edition: 2011.

Scripture quotations marked KJV are taken from *The King James Version*.

Scripture quotations marked NKJV are taken from the *New King James Version*. Copyright © 1982 by Thomas Nelson, Inc. Used by permission. All rights reserved.

Copyright © Tom Nettles 2021

paperback ISBN 978-1-5271-0648-2
epub ISBN 978-1-5271-0747-2
mobi ISBN 978-1-5271-0748-9

10 9 8 7 6 5 4 3 2 1

Published in 2021
by
Christian Focus Publications Ltd,
Geanies House, Fearn, Ross-shire,
IV20 1TW, Great Britain.

www.christianfocus.com

Cover design by
Daniel van Straaten

Cover illustration from
The Print Collector / Alamy Stock Photo

Printed and bound by Bell & Bain

CONTENTS

ABBREVIATIONS

Lectures Lectures to My Students

MTP Metropolitan Tabernacle Pulpit

NPSP New Park Street Pulpit

S&T Sword and Trowel magazine

SEE Spurgeon's Expository Encyclopedia

SS Sermons of Rev. C. H. Spurgeon

INTRODUCTION
• • • • • • • • • • • • • • • • • •

A Rev. Mr Mood wrote an article for The Southern Christian Advocate in 1857 entitled 'The Modern Whitefield'. This was a Methodist publication, but it was reprinted by *The Southern Baptist* on 2 June 1857. After a narration concerning the size of the venue at the Surrey Gardens Music Hall, the difficulty of obtaining tickets, and the press of the crowd, Mr Mood described the singing by 10,000 people. The Modern Whitefield had announced the hymn by Watts, 'Come Ye that Love the Lord,' in a 'clear, full, silvery voice.' The congregation sang. This modern Whitefield, Charles Spurgeon, prayed and announced another hymn, 'Grace, 'tis a Charming Sound.' He read from Psalm 84. As he read, 'The speaker makes a few simple and on the whole, appropriate comments.' But again, how wonderfully adapted is the voice for rapt attention! 'Listen to the voice and observe the well chosen gestures. His voice fills the house, and though you are seated at the farthest end of the Hall, every syllable is distinctly heard.'

The writer recorded the four-point sermon outline from Psalm 106:8: 'Nevertheless, He saved them for His name's sake.' First, who saved them; second, who is it that is saved; third, why are they saved; and fourth, what is implied in 'nevertheless'. Mood remarked about the well-chosen manner of gesturing, noted the utter quiet of the congregation during the presentation, with a brief respite for coughing and shifting position after the completion of each point. Mood remarked that Spurgeon was 'bold in his enumeration and denunciation of sin and holds up the cross throughout.'

The service closed with singing the doxology. 'All sing,' Mood noted, 'and you leave the house with a thankful and improved heart.' He observed that 'Mr Spurgeon is a remarkable instance of the power of voice and action.' And while Mood opined within the theme of many of the critical papers of London that 'His sermons, in composition, are surpassed by several hundred ministers every Sabbath, in the very city in which he preaches,' he added the remarkable truth, 'but while many of them fail to get a tolerable congregation, no house can be found large enough to accommodate his audience.'[1]

Thirty-one years later, William E. Hatcher had a visit with Spurgeon for five hours on a Saturday afternoon in 1888. The Downgrade Controversy had already brought a censure on Spurgeon and his resignation from the Baptist Union. Hatcher, along with two companions, caught a ride from the Crystal Palace to Beulah Hill, Spurgeon's home in Upper Norwood. Everything about the home was impressive – its size, its location, its gardens, its pastures and animals, its flowers and trees, its stables and horses and carriages, its statuary, its lakes and streams, its vegetable garden, and its milk cows – and gave Hatcher a moment of astonishment 'to find that he lived in such magnificence and elegance'. Soon he learned of how Spurgeon came to acquire the property, how its grand appearance caused Spurgeon anxiety, how he used it to produce income for the many ministries of the Tabernacle, and how it would become a major source of funding for these ministries after the death of the Spurgeons.

Conversation was both lively and serious, jocular and melancholy, and was developed along a walk through the grounds that ended with a discussion in the summer house. When the Downgrade entered the discussion, Hatcher observed 'a sober and even pathetic tone in his conversation on the subject'. Spurgeon, contrary to reports in America, had not ceased to be a Baptist, 'but he simply

---

1. Mood, 'The Modern Whitefield,' *The Southern Baptist*, 2 June 1857, p. 2.

declines to stay in an organization which appears to be too tolerant of error.' They stayed for tea. Afterwards, a brief time of worship in Spurgeon's study where 'the reading was rendered delightful and impressive by his expository comments' brought an encouraging and edifying end to this Saturday visit. They left at 6:00 pm, for that was the time when Spurgeon began work on his sermons for the next day. In closing the narrative, Hatcher gave an extensive observation.

> We departed from Beulah Hill in a glow of happiness. It was something to be thankful for that we had spent five hours in pleasant companionship with the world's most famous preacher, but far better was the hallowing spiritual charm of the man himself. He lives upon the mountain, and the transfiguring light is upon his face. It is impossible to touch him without receiving the thrill of his holy power. We felt as if we had been to a revival and had gotten nearer to the Lord. It was a privilege cherished and priceless, which I could not hope would come again. Happily for me, it was only the beginning of yet more delightful experiences which I was destined to enjoy in the company of Mr Spurgeon.[2]

A thirty-one year expanse that moves from mere, but appreciatively satisfied, curiosity to a sense of privilege in the presence of a man, from one whose sermon composition was less impressive than a hundred other nearby preachers to the estimation that this one is the 'world's most famous preacher', from the reality that controversy involves the willingness to confront to the sense that one's presence manifests a transcendent spiritual ambience – this phenomenon begs for some analytical explanation. This book, as a companion to my larger biography of Spurgeon, is an attempt to isolate several key and consistent factors that developed from youth to old age in harmony with each other and molded Spurgeon into the charming, interesting, confident, humble, spiritual-minded man and pastor whose work and witness dominated evangelicalism during the

---

2. William E. Hatcher, 'An Evening with Spurgeon,' *The Baptist Courier*, 24 January 1889, p. 1.

last half of the nineteenth century. *The Child is Father of the Man* traces ten key convictions that appeared before or immediately after Spurgeon's conversion, matured in power and clarity throughout his ministry, and consistently disciplined him for an 'All-Round Ministry' as an all-round preacher.

1

THE CHILD IS FATHER OF THE MAN

My heart leaps up when I behold
A rainbow in the sky:
So was it when my life began;
So is it now I am a man;
So be it when I shall grow old,
Or let me die!
The Child is father of the Man;
I could wish my days to be
Bound each to each by natural piety.

When Charles Spurgeon reviewed a biography of William Wordsworth by A. J. Symington in 1881, he described as a strength of Wordsworth an intuitionism characteristic of himself. Wordsworth's power lay in his 'sympathy with the spirit which is embodied in visible things, and in his perception of the moral teaching of all things that are.' Spurgeon's own love for nature and his commitment to see natural phenomena as brimming with spiritual application and illustration of doctrine[1] made him more friendly

---

1. As an example of Spurgeon's use of nature for substantial sermonic material, see his *Teachings of Nature in the Kingdom of Grace* (London: Passmore and Alabaster, 1896). This book, containing fifty-six selections of articles, sermons, and brief essays, does not move from nature to sermon but from a biblical text that has some reference to a natural phenomenon into an exposition of how the gospel employs that natural phenomenon as an apt illustration of spiritual truth.

toward and grateful for this insight than Wordsworth's mystical intuitism could have prompted in itself.[2] Given his understanding of providence Spurgeon would agree that 'The Child is Father of the Man' and also that our days are 'bound each to each', not so much by a 'natural piety' as by divine purpose, perceived most clearly in gospel-wrought piety.

In 1874 he cited a Wordsworth phrase as having spiritual insight to prompt the 'enlargement of the sphere of our life'. Wordsworth wrote of the farmer, enmeshed in natural wonder in every stage of his vocation, who has no sight for its transcendent beauty:

> The primrose by the river's brim
> A yellow primrose was to him,
> And nothing more!

Plowing and sowing, reaping and mowing, constituted the farmer's philosophy and prompted 'no sacred homilies to him; the birds sang, but he would have been as much pleased if they had been silent; the hills were a weariness to climb, and the view from their summit he thought nothing of; his soul was inside his smock frock and his corduroys, and he never wished to go beyond them.'

Spurgeon believed that the cities also were filled with such men who found the 'music of the spheres' in the clink of sovereigns. Their souls are 'like squirrels in cages, and each day their wheel revolves.' Christ came to give His people 'a wider, broader life than this.' Many merely natural men see insightfully into the wonders of nature and are deep in philosophy 'and force their way into the secret chambers where the immature principles of things are nestling.'

Still, however, they are bound by time and space. But new life in Jesus 'enlarges the sphere of the most capacious mind, and makes the greatest intellect to feel' that before knowing Christ his understanding was 'cabined, cribbed, [and] confined.' When one has been 'tossed upon the stormy sea of sin, and has descended

---

2. S&T, August 1881, p. 417.

into the deeps of the tremendous ocean of terror,' the 'grace of our pardoning God' has given us a new world. When we can see His smile, feast on His love, and have fellowship with the infinite, 'We are no longer shut up to self, but we hold conversation with the spirits before the throne of God and commune with all the saints redeemed by blood!' Now we have seen mysteries which 'were before hidden from our eyes!'[3]

Even so, when one has a merely cognitive knowledge of biblical truth and an external acquaintance with spiritual realities, he is no less 'cabined, cribbed, [and] confined.' He must be given new sight to blind eyes and spiritual clues to unlock revealed mysteries. When his eyes were opened, already so much lay before his sight that progress was immediate and rapid. Spurgeon observed: 'I suppose all the powers of the man are in the child, but many of them are dormant, and will only be exercised when life is more abundant.' Among several keys to the full exercise of resident powers is fitting knowledge: 'Life is in their hearts, ... but it is only partially in their heads, for they do not study the gospel nor use their brains to understand its truths.'[4] For Spurgeon, the brain was loaded before the heart had life.

The Expansive Possibility of Early Preparation

When eyes are opened, they must be opened to see things that are there. The more that is there, the more one sees. Depth of knowledge more quickly becomes settled maturity and expansive usefulness. Early training will bear abundant fruit.

The advantages of early preparation can be seen with power in the history of the apostle Paul. He states that 'I was advancing in Judaism beyond many of my own age among my people, so extremely zealous was I for the traditions of my fathers' (Gal. 1:14). Paul's knowledge of the Old Testament and his grasp of the received

---

3. MTP 20:1150: 'Life More Abundant.'
4. Ibid.

interpretations exceeded that of any of his contemporaries. Then, reflecting on the relationship between divine sovereignty in salvation and the immediate effects of his intellectual life, he reported: 'But when he who had set me apart before I was born, and who called me by his grace, was pleased to reveal his Son to me, in order that I might preach him among the Gentiles, I did not immediately consult with anyone, ... but I went away into Arabia' (Gal. 1:16-17).

Paul went there for a twofold purpose: one, called with striking certainty as an apostle, he went to receive the revelation of the new covenant as consisting of the person and work of Christ – 'was pleased to reveal his Son to me.' This happened with greater profundity and depth than to any other apostle (2 Pet. 3:15; 1 Cor. 3:10, 11; 4:1, 15). Two, this revelation would be given in accord with the knowledge that he already had of the revelation constituting the Old Testament. His scheme of interpretation was radically altered, but the knowledge he already had attained rendered his usefulness greatly expanded. For this reason, very soon Paul 'proclaimed Jesus in the synagogues, saying, "He is the Son of God,"' and 'increased all the more in strength, and confounded the Jews who lived in Damascus by proving that Jesus was the Christ' (Acts 9:20, 22).

When Paul counted 'everything as loss' he was not rejecting the value of his deep knowledge of Scripture or of the righteousness set forth in the Law. He had not seen it in the light of Christ and, therefore, when Christ was revealed to him, both in the saving encounter and in the radical reorientation of biblical interpretation, every gain he formerly had both in righteousness and knowledge and supposed ethnic purity came to be nothing in and of itself. Instead, 'the surpassing worth of knowing Christ Jesus' replaced and reinterpreted all of it.

Even so, the early preparation of Spurgeon in doctrinal knowledge and expectations of piety, when placed in the light of the saving work of Christ, flowered into incomparable power and consistency in his calling as a pastor. An American biographer, daring to make a judgment when Spurgeon was but twenty-three years old, in 1857 wrote:

Before he left Cambridge, while the dignitaries of the university and town were enjoying their lettered content, Mr Spurgeon was wont frequently to address Sunday Schools, in season and out of season; to visit the neighboring villages, where descending day, as well as opening morn, found him still busy in refreshing the weary and spiritually destitute. Thus, in the very morning of his life, in the dew of his youth, we find him in labors more abundant, his ardor and love supplying the lack of experience, and filling his friends with the highest hopes of his future usefulness and fame, in the service of his Divine Master.[5]

Immediately upon his conversion, and even before, Spurgeon began manifesting several characteristics that would be prominent in his entire Christian pilgrimage. He saw this truth about himself and gloried in the power of these early impressions: 'For one, I bless God that I knew the doctrines of grace from my youth; they have been the staff of my manhood, and I believe they will be the glory of my old age. So far from being ashamed of the election of grace, it commands the enthusiasm of my whole being.'[6]

Principled Commitment to Providence

Spurgeon saw everything in light of the divine purpose and measured his response externally and internally in light of biblical doctrine. In an early sermon on providence Spurgeon, reflecting on the vision of the wheels in Ezekiel, said: 'The eye of God is everywhere; Providence is universal.' Again, he emphasized, 'In all seasons, at all times, in all dangers, and in all climates, there is the hand of God.' Even to the end of history and into eternity, all events are 'forever fixed by the eternal decree of the mighty God'. These events include the most apparently inconsequential things to those that are most powerful and devastating. 'The creeping of an aphis over the rosebud is as much fixed as the march of the devastating pestilence – the fall of sere leaves from a poplar is as fully ordained as the tumbling of an avalanche.'[7]

---

5. SS 1:vii.
6. SEE 7:35.
7. SS 2:194, 197, 201.

One year after his baptism, he wrote his mother, reminding her that even difficulties came to her as a result of the eternal covenant of grace and that she should not wish to retrace any step. 'Mark the providences of this year; how clearly have you seen His hand in things which others esteem chance! God, who has moved the world, has exercised His own vast heart and thought for you. All your life, your spiritual life, all things have worked together for good; nothing has gone wrong, for God has directed, controlled all.'

In his remarks on Matthew 10:29-31, Spurgeon noted the intricate detail of God's providence toward His people. Even as their very hairs are numbered, 'to the most minute circumstance, all their lives are under the arrangement of the Lord of love. Chance is not our creed; the decree of the Eternal Watcher rules our destiny, and love is seen in every line of that decree.'[8] Spurgeon was committed to reflection on formative providential arrangements in his life.

Providential Arrangements of Early Life

He was born in Essex, in the village of Kelvedon, on 19 June 1834.[9] His parents were John and Eliza Jarvis Spurgeon. He was the first of seventeen children, only eight of whom survived infancy. He went to live with his grandfather, James Spurgeon, an independent minister in Stambourne,[10] for more than four years, returning to Colchester in 1840. His grandmother, Sarah, and aunt, eighteen-year-old Ann, surrounded him with affection and favor, putting fresh-baked cookies on the bottom shelf for the child. He also had access to a rocking horse so steady that even a member of Parliament could keep his seat. For years Spurgeon went back frequently during summers and school breaks.

He recalled the joyful fellowship between his grandfather and the Parish minister, Mr Hopkins, on Mondays. Tea, warm cinnamon

---

8. *Matthew*, p. 74
9. Kelvedon is a village in the county of Essex, located between Chelmsford and Colchester.
10. Stambourne is also a village in Essex.

bread, and savory spiritual talk gave indelible impressions of oneness in Christ. The social standing of ecclesiastical position dissolved before the leveling and exalting power of true gospel faith. Also the necessity of a visible manifestation of true communion between all the redeemed influenced Spurgeon's view of the Lord's Supper.

Spurgeon learned at Stambourne, as well as at home, that sermon preparation time was of preeminent importance. He could watch, but he must not talk or distract in any way, because faithfulness to God's glory and the souls of men was at stake in the spiritual sensitivity which gave birth to a sermon.

He also received a permanent commitment to the beauty and power of the old writers. His love for and acquaintance with the Puritans developed among the shelves of a library of Puritan books that had been left to the manse for the minister of the Dissenters' congregation. The room was darkened because the windows had been plastered due to a tax on houses according to their number of windows. Spurgeon did not understand the policy of taxing the light, but he received more than enough compensation of doctrinal light in the company of the books. Here he lived in the pages and walked all the paths of *Pilgrim's Progress*. Here, in Foxe's *Book of Martyrs,* he saw the horror of religious persecution as well as the power of the blood of martyrs sown as seed on a land. He loved the covers of the books themselves, for like harassed saints of old they went around in sheepskins and goatskins. The covers were great but the contents better as he became familiar with the works of Sibbes, Brooks, Owen, Henry and others. The Puritans became the context by which he judged both the faithfulness and the maturity of doctrinal commitment. Departures from Puritan piety and thought was sufficient evidence of creeping skepticism and doctrinal infidelity in Spurgeon's view. In his sermon 'Faith,' preached at Surrey Gardens in December 1856, Spurgeon told the massive crowd gathered from all over London: 'The old writers, who are by far the most sensible, – for you will notice, that the books that were written about two hundred years ago by the old

Puritans have more sense in one line than there is in a page of our new books, and more in a page than there is in a whole volume of our modern divinity.'[11]

He also learned to respect the spiritually pungent observations made by disciplined Christians about everyday events of life. He developed his perennially favorite character John Ploughman from taking note of, and perhaps notes from, his own grandfather and a town wit named Will Richardson who was famous for his 'crip' sayings. 'I hate to hear a raven croak at a crow for being black.'

An early fascination with the reward of hymn memorizing began under the influence of his grandmother. Both the man and the woman of the senior Spurgeons made promises to 'the boy'. A shilling for a dozen rats from his grandfather was the deal from the distinguished pastor; a penny per hymn from his grandmother. He knew which was most immediately profitable monetarily. He learned hymns so quickly that his grandmother had to reduce the rate of pay, but there was an abundance of rats to be found in the acres around the property. He learned that, even at a reduced rate, hymn-learning far transcended rat-killing spiritually. 'No matter on what topic I am preaching,' Spurgeon reflected, 'I can even now, in the middle of any sermon, quote some verse of a hymn in harmony with the subject. The hymns have remained with me.'[12] Augustus Toplady, William Cowper, John Newton, and Isaac Watts were particularly resonant with both his theology and his literary taste. To give a seal to a point in his first sermon in the *New Park Street Pulpit,* 'The immutability of God,' Spurgeon quoted sections from six hymns. In speaking of the unchangeableness of God's eternal covenant of redemption, Spurgeon gave an emotional seal to his argument by citation of the verse of a popular hymn:

> God alters not His plans, why should He? He is Almighty and there-
> fore can perform His pleasure. Why should He? He is the All-wise

---

11. SS 1:366.
12. *Autobiography*, 1:44.

and therefore cannot have planned wrongly. Why should He? He is the everlasting God and therefore cannot die before His plan is accomplished. Why should He change? You worthless atoms of existence, ephemera of the day! you creeping insects upon this bay-leaf of existence! you may change your plans, but He shall never, never change His. Then has He told me that His plan is to save me? If so, I am safe –

> My name from the palms of His hands
> Eternity will not erase;
> Impress'd on His heart it remains,
> In marks of indelible grace.

Two of Toplady's hymns appear often as quotes in his sermons. From 'Rock of Ages', Spurgeon frequently would quote:

> Nothing in my hand I bring,
> Simply to thy cross I cling.

From 'Whence This Fear and Unbelief,' Spurgeon focused on the certainty of the atoning work of Christ's substitutionary death in these words:

> Payment God cannot twice demand
> First at my bleeding surety's hand
> And then again at mine.

Spurgeon edited a hymn book for his congregation at the Metropolitan Tabernacle, publishing it in 1866. Including the Psalms, *Our Own Hymnbook* contained 1,060 hymns.

Prophecy, Conviction, Conversion

When Spurgeon was ten and visiting his grandfather, Richard Knill on deputation from the London Missionary Society stayed for three days in the manse. Knill was deeply impressed with the comments and questions of the ten-year-old boy. He arranged to pray with Spurgeon on three mornings at 6:00 a.m. Before he left, he predicted that Spurgeon would preach to large crowds and one day would preach in the chapel of Rowland Hill. To give substance to this prophecy, he extracted from Spurgeon a promise to memorize 'God Moves in a Mysterious Way His Wonders to Perform' and to have it sung when he preached in the chapel. Things happened as Knill said, and Spurgeon preached in both of Hill's chapels, on each occasion having the designated hymn sung. 'To me,' Spurgeon commented, 'it was a very wonderful thing, and I no more understand to-day why the Lord should be so gracious to me.'[13]

Soon after the Knill encounter, he came under increasingly severe conviction for sin. He endured five years of intense conviction as 'God's law was flogging me with its ten-thonged whip, and then rubbing me with brine afterwards, so that I did shake and quiver with pain and anguish.' His conscience also testified against him. 'Our heavenly Father does not usually cause us to seek the Saviour till He has whipped us clean out of all our confidence; He cannot make us in earnest after heaven till He has made us feel something of the intolerable tortures of an aching conscience, which is a foretaste of hell.'

His mother prayed for him, taught him, and warned him. He confessed that he did not have the powers of speech to give sufficient gratitude for 'the choice blessing which the Lord bestowed on me in making me the son of one who prayed for, and prayed with me.' Prayers not only comforted but alarmed him, for his mother would end by saying, 'Now, Lord, if my children go on in their sins, it will not be from ignorance that they perish, and my soul must bear witness against them at the day of judgment if they lay not hold of Christ.' Those words, Spurgeon testified, 'pierced my conscience, and stirred my heart.'[14]

Later Spurgeon would remember those days of intercession and state the effect as a settled conviction:

> Furthermore, it is not necessary, still it may strengthen the point, if we
> add that our own experience leads us to believe that God will answer

---

13. *Memories of Stambourne*, p. 104.
14. *Autobiography*, 1:44.

prayer. I must not speak for you, but I may speak for myself. If there be anything I know, anything that I am quite assured of beyond all question, it is that praying breath is never spent in vain. If no other man here can say it, I dare to say it and I know that I can prove it. My own conversion is the result of prayer – long, affectionate, earnest, importunate. Parents prayed for me. God heard their cries and here I am to preach the Gospel.[15]

In 1848, he went to school in Maidstone for one year.[16] He recalled a discussion with an Anglican vicar over baptism. When the vicar sought to have Spurgeon submit to the correctness of baptism in the established church and pressed him to pursue it, Spurgeon responded: 'Oh no! I have been baptized once, before I ought; I will wait next time till I am fit for it.' In later reflections, Spurgeon wryly reported, 'It is due to the Church of England catechism that I am a Baptist.' Though changed in his view of baptism, he still was unchanged in heart.

In August of 1849, Spurgeon moved to Newmarket,[17] where he assisted J. D. Everett as an assistant tutor. They became good friends as well as roommates. Everett described Spurgeon as 'rather small and delicate, with pale but plump face, dark brown eyes and hair, and a bright, lively manner, with a never-failing flow of conversation.'[18] Everett knew that Spurgeon had been raised with 'Puritan tendencies' but was not privy to the inner turmoil that he was enduring. He still was seeking right standing before a holy God.

His conversion took place on 6 January 1850. Though some have challenged the date due to meteorological evidence, I think it is safe to trust Spurgeon's recollection. He had been unable to go with his father to his preaching assignment, so, in the midst of a snowstorm, he stumbled into a Primitive Methodist Chapel in Colchester. Spurgeon refers to this throughout his ministry, giving

---

15. MTP 11:619: 'The Golden Key of Prayer.'
16. Maidstone is located in the county of Kent.
17. Newmarket is a town in the county of Suffolk.
18. Pike, 1:39.

its implications in different contexts of preaching. In the absence of the regular minister, a layman took the pulpit and preached from Isaiah 45:22. From that text, the layman preached for several minutes on Jesus as the spat-upon, scourged, crucified, buried, risen, ascended, and interceding Savior. Then he singled Spurgeon out from among the sparse group of attendees, pointed to him, and called on him to heed the words of Jesus, 'Look unto me!' That evening, Spurgeon spoke to his father about this and told him, 'In the text, "Look, look, look," I found salvation this morning. In the text, "Accepted in the Beloved," preached at the Baptist church in the evening, I found peace and pardon.'[19] Spurgeon looked, had been accepted, his life was changed – and the English-speaking world was changed.

Called and Equipped

After his conversion, Spurgeon kept his word concerning baptism. After a tense delay in receiving permission from his father, he was baptized on 3 May 1850, on his mother's birthday, by a Mr Cantlow at Isleham.[20] He testified that his timidity left him in that event and loosed his tongue. Spurgeon had been for almost a year as a sub-tutor in a school at Newmarket run by Mr Swindell. Probably during his first term he had had a bout with philosophical skepticism and had experienced its mental and emotional ravages. Also, he came to know a sturdy woman, Mary King, that the students referred to as 'Cook'. From her, Spurgeon learned to enjoy the pithy, experiential conversation of a deeply committed Calvinist and also how earnest church members searched for good in the minister's sermons. He confessed unashamedly that she had taught him his theology, and, subsequent to his conversion she provided even more profound encouragement. At winter break, he had his saving confrontation with the Primitive Methodist preacher.

---

19. Pike, 1:36.
20. Isleham is a small village in the county of Cambridgeshire.

On returning to Newmarket, Spurgeon began to distribute tracts on Saturday. He wrote his mother in February, 'I have 33 houses at present where I leave tracts.' By June he distributed tracts to seventy people regularly. He sat down with them and sought to press them to note the important spiritual realities involved in the words. Also, he worked in the Sunday School. He taught a class of boys, and soon spent his late afternoons teaching the other Sunday School teachers.

In the late summer of 1850, under the encouragement and influence of his father, Spurgeon moved to Cambridge to the school of Charles Leeding, a teacher he had had in Colchester. Again, he was a student as well as a tutor. He joined St. Andrews Baptist Church that had once been served by Robert Robinson as pastor. The church had survived his journey from orthodoxy to Socinianism and it provided a place for Spurgeon, giving him the opportunity for continued ministry in Sunday School teaching. Several were impressed with his teaching, predicted an influential future for him, while others felt his confident demeanor, strong doctrinal convictions, and boldness of presentation were rude and brash in one so young. It would not be the last time Spurgeon would need to shoulder criticism.

The church also had a Lay Preachers' Association. James Vinter was its guiding light. Aware of the ability of Spurgeon in public discourse and confident in his religious experience and doctrinal soundness, Vinter arranged, unknown to Spurgeon, for him to preach at Teversham. He told Spurgeon that a young man unaccustomed to preach was to do so at Teversham and would be in need of company. Would Spurgeon be willing to make the trip to Teversham? Of course. Along the way, Spurgeon discovered that his traveling mate had never preached, had no intention of preaching, and if Spurgeon did not preach, there would be no sermon for the people. Besides, he continued, you regularly teach Sunday School. The cottage congregation in Teversham would benefit from one of the lessons recently taught. For the rest of the walk Spurgeon thought through 'Therefore, to you who believe, He is precious' (1 Pet. 2:7 NKJV). He preached – introduction, development of points, and close. As he began the closing hymn, an older woman interrupted, 'Bless your dear heart. How old are you?' He mildly rebuked the question, led in the hymn and then told the inquisitor that he was under sixty, to which she responded, 'Yes, and under sixteen.'

The Lay Preachers' Association itinerations took Spurgeon to many villages and stirred increasingly intense interest in the boy preacher. One of these journeys led to a church where he spent the afternoon in debate with Potto Brown, the zealous Finneyite, the wealthy 'miller of Houghton'.

A Pastor

In the middle of October 1851, the seventeen-year-old Spurgeon wrote his father about a 'place called Waterbeach, where there is an old-established Church, but not able to support a minister.' They were much like the people at Stambourne and immediately they were attached to Spurgeon and he was to them. He resigned his position in Cambridge and moved to Waterbeach.[21] The church experienced numerical growth and spiritual revival; the town underwent a social and moral transformation. There he heard of and then spoke to the first person converted under his preaching. The thrill of such a seal on his ministry could not be transcended. Thousands of others would yet come, but the first was the needed seal and the cause of Spurgeon's own unending *Magnificat*.

Several observers of Spurgeon's talents desired that he go to Stepney College, a school of training for Baptist ministers. Spurgon's father concurred. In pursuit of that, Dr Joseph Angus scheduled a meeting with Spurgeon in the home of the publisher MacMillan. Through a bizarre miscommunication of the young maid responsible for welcoming guests, Angus and Spurgeon were

---

21. Waterbeach is a village six miles north of Cambridge.

put into separate rooms and never had their meeting. On his way from the house back to Waterbeach, Spurgeon had an experience in which he determined that he would not seek a college education.

Crossing Midsummer Common, contemplating a future of learning and recognition, and thinking of an action that would 'leave my poor people in the wilderness that I might become something great', a verse came to him: 'Seek you great things for yourself? Seek them not.' In that moment he decided not to pursue the change.[22] He wrote his father, asking him to determine the case for him but offering his own opinion that he would prefer to stay at Waterbeach. Among the four weighty reasons he gave his father he said, 'Providence has thrown me into a great sphere of usefulness, – a congregation of often 450, a loving and praying church, and an awakened audience. Many already own that the preaching has been with power from heaven. Now, ought I to leave them?'[23]

He did not. But in December 1853, being then nineteen years of age, he was invited by letter to preach in London at the New Park Street Chapel. Upon first receiving the letter, he was sure it had been delivered to him by mistake, but must be for some relative of his. His faithful deacon, Mr Coe, assured him the invitation was intended for him; Coe knew that such a day would come soon. The church had been founded in 1652. Among others who had served that church as pastor, Benjamin Keach did for thirty-six years, John Gill for fifty-one years, and John Rippon for sixty-three years. Joseph Angus had succeeded Rippon for four years. With heavy heart and dread, Spurgeon obeyed the summons and went to London to do his duty on 18 December 1853.

After a miserable and intimidating night in a boarding house on Queen Square, Spurgeon found his way to New Park Street. The congregation that morning was a mere handful. The chapel seemed large and gloomy. But he went to his task, preaching on James 1:17.

22. NPSP 4:215: 'His Name: Counsellor.'
23. Murray, *Letters*, p. 36.

The evening saw a significantly increased attendance for a sermon on 'They are without fault before the throne of God'. He was asked to return on the first, third, and fifth Sundays in January 1854. Before the last of these he received an invitation, dated 25 January, inviting him to a six-month trial. He countered, offering a three-month trial. Before the three months were over, the church gave him an invitation to come as pastor, with prayer for 'an outpouring of the Holy Spirit and a revival of religion in our midst; that it may be fruitful in the conversion of sinners, and in the edification of those that believe.' With confidence in divine leadership, Spurgeon accepted.

One evening in 1854, Spurgeon called for the falling of the back walls of the Chapel like the walls of Jericho, for expansion of the building. His prudent insistence on the project led to an expansion and renovation of New Park Street Chapel. Consequently, while this was being done, the church met for worship at Exeter Hall, from 11 February to 27 May 1855. Exeter Hall was thronged throughout this period. Scathing opposition to Spurgeon during this time made him more famous than infamous, and that expanded venue was insufficient to hold the crowds desiring to hear him. Even the renovated chapel now was insufficient to hold the crowds.

By August 1856, plans were underway for the construction of an entirely new edifice. On 16 October, services began at the Royal Surrey Gardens. The tragedy, promulgated by lawless, unprincipled, villainous people yelling 'Fire' and other warnings of danger, led to a panic that killed seven people and injured twenty-eight others. Spurgeon was devastated and compelled to stop preaching. He resumed on Sunday, 31 October, and by degrees recovered both his physical and mental health.

By January 1859, money was in hand to purchase the land at Elephant and Castle, the site of the new construction. The first stone of the Metropolitan Tabernacle was laid on 16 August 1859. The congregation left the Surrey Music Hall in December because of a disagreement over use of the facility for amusements on the Lord's Day. They began, for the third time, to occupy Exeter Hall on

18 December 1859. This ended on 31 March 1861, when he preached the last service at Exeter Hall and then preached in the evening in the completed Metropolitan Tabernacle, a debt-free facility.

Two weeks of services inaugurated the ministries that would only increase in number and effectiveness through the years. A Baptist night was held on 2 April; on 3 April was held a public meeting of 'various denominations'. On 4 April, Octavius Winslow preached on 'Christ's Finished Work'. On Sunday 7 April, Spurgeon preached on 'Perfect Cleansing'. On Monday 8 April saw a 'Meeting of our Own Church' with speakers from the past and present giving fitting remarks. On 9 April, Hugh Stowell Brown preached on 'Christian Baptism'. On 11 April, the day was devoted to an exposition of the doctrines of grace.

Mr Henry Vincent spoke the following evening on 'Nonconformity'. He closed his eloquent and moving oration with this flourish:

> Bear about you the marks of this ancient glory. Never sully your ancient principles. March on, knowing that until the last vestige of ecclesiastical wrong is dead, until liberty is enjoyed by all states, that you have a glorious work to do, and God shall bless you, and sanctify and make you a blessing, until the fulness of all nations shall come, and the Spirit of the Lord be poured forth in triumphant power upon all lands, to consume all foulness, and fill the earth with light, and love, and liberty.[24]

The congregation, led by their twenty-seven-year-old pastor, began regular work at the Tabernacle in May 1861. Evangelical convictions, in a Calvinistic orientation, would inform all that was done. The building was debt free and would become the scene of an expansive ministry of preaching, evangelism, benevolence, and education unparalleled by any local church in evangelical Christianity. The child was father of the man. In how many ways his days 'were bound each to each' in fervent biblically-informed piety, we shall now investigate.

---

24. MTP 7:344: 'Nonconformity.'

2

'THE STAFF OF MY MANHOOD, THE GLORY OF MY OLD AGE'
••••••••••••••••••••••••••••••••

Virtually synchronic to his conversion, Spurgeon held a clear conviction concerning the doctrines of grace and God's eternal covenantal pursuit of His people. 'For one,' so he testified to his congregation in 1884, 'I bless God that I knew the doctrines of grace from my youth; they have been the staff of my manhood, and I believe they will be the glory of my old age. So far from being ashamed of the election of grace, it commands the enthusiasm of my whole being.' Nor did he want them hid from children. 'It is said by some,' Spurgeon reflected, 'that children cannot understand the great mysteries of religion. We even know some Sunday-school teachers who cautiously avoid mentioning the great doctrines of the gospel because they think the children are not prepared to receive them.' Based on his experience and the example of the Word of God, Spurgeon wanted children 'taught all the great doctrines of truth without a solitary exception, that they may in their after days hold fast by them.'[1]

G. Holden Pike wrote, concerning Spurgeon at Newmarket: 'The doctrines he then embraced were such as remained dear to him until the end.' They were identical to those held by his

---

1. *Autobiography*, 1:45, 46.

grandfather and father and 'from the great truths themselves, he never swerved.'[2]

This deeply felt companionship of truth prompted him to encourage his congregation not to hide or pass by these doctrines in their evangelistic witness.[3] Spurgeon regarded this an attempt to hide the truth and considered it 'priestcraft' and 'Jesuitical'. All that God has revealed should be preached and also taught. Nothing should be withheld by justifying omissions by mental reservation. Though he had heard these doctrines clearly expounded for years before the evening at the Primitive Methodist Chapel in Colchester, his experience of opened-eyes confirmed in a moment what he had heard all his life. For him, those doctrines highlighted the freeness of divine mercy, gave security to the tender Christian conscience, and guaranteed a harvest of souls in evangelism.

Early Recognition of Indebtedness to Grace

Conversion

To his father Spurgeon wrote, 'Were it not all of sovereign, electing, almighty grace, I, for one, could never hope to be saved.'[4] He frequently reflected on the personal dimensions of his being a debtor to mercy alone. Grace had claimed him in eternity past and was exhibited in his experience of conviction and conversion. Preaching in 1855, Spurgeon described with striking images the internal operation of grace at his conversion that worked side by side with the external providential arrangement that made him look to Jesus. He described how he felt the power in his mind and heart and how palpably grace arrested him in his descent to greater hardness against the gospel:

> Once I, like Mazeppa, bound on the wild horse of my lust, bound hand
> and foot, incapable of resistance, was galloping on with hell's wolves
> behind me, howling for my body and soul, as their just and lawful
> prey. There came a mighty hand which stopped that wild horse, cut

2. Pike, 1:42.
3. SEE 7:35.
4. Murray, *Letters*, p. 24.

my bands, set me down, and brought me into liberty. Is there power, sir? Aye, there is power; and he who has felt it must acknowledge it.

He described 'the strong old castle of my sins' and his attempt at works righteousness. 'A trumpeter' (the many sermons that he heard from faithful preachers) came to the door of his heart, but young Spurgeon 'with anger chid him from the porch, and said he ne'er should enter.' But then, 'a goodly personage, with loving countenance' came. This One had hands that 'were marked with scars, where nails were driven' and His feet also bore the marks of cruel crucifixion. He used His cross 'as a hammer' and smashed his prejudice with a single blow. Another blow shook him even more, and finally, 'at the third down it fell, and in he came.' The crucified One with the weapon of the cross commanded Spurgeon to stand to his feet, and announced: 'I have loved thee with an everlasting love.' Spurgeon applied the image, 'A thing of power! Ah! It is a thing of power. I have felt it *here*, in this heart; I have the witness of the Spirit within, and know it is a thing of might because it has conquered me; it has bowed me down.'[5]

On another occasion, writing of the same series of blows to his conscience, Spurgeon said: 'When my heart was a little touched, I tried to divert it with sinful pleasures, and would not then have been saved, until God gave me the effectual blow, and I was obliged to submit to that irresistible effort of His grace.' He maintained the image of conquering in continuing: 'It conquered my depraved will, and made me bow myself before His gracious scepter.' The power of the effectual blow he described: 'He sent one great shot which shivered me to pieces; and, lo I found myself utterly defenceless.'[6]

Sanctifying Power

'An everlasting love' – that thought drove him forward and occupied his thoughts constantly. Having heard a sermon on 1 Corinthians 4:7

---

5. SS 1:104-05. For this same sermon, see NPSP 1855: 57, 58.
6. *Autobiography*, 1:71.

he reflected: 'Truly, I have nothing which I have not received; I can boast of no inherent righteousness. Had the Lord not chosen me, I should not have chosen Him.' Given the hardened state of human sin and the consequent absolute dependence on effectual converting power, Spurgeon's joy in contemplating the divine initiative constantly occupied his young thoughts and never lost its glow for him. 'Grace! Grace! Grace! 'Tis all of grace,' he exclaimed with ink and paper. 'I can do nothing, I am less than nothing,' he admitted, but not to ultimate despair. 'Yet what a difference – once a slave of hell, now the son of the God of Heaven! Help me to walk worthy of my lofty and exalted vocation!'[7]

These pivotal doctrines, embracing covenantal operations of each person of the triune God, undergirded Spurgeon's spiritual confidence and established an immovable structure of security in all the challenges of life and ministry from the first day of his conversion until his death. In 1850, for example, he wrote his father that he had been 'unwell in body'. At the same time, his 'soul has been almost in Heaven'. He had seen his title clear and knew that 'sooner than one of God's little ones shall perish, God Himself will cease to be, Satan will conquer the King of kings, and Jesus will no longer be the Savior of the elect.' Any doubts and fears ordained by His gracious heavenly Father will pose no dread to him, since, even above the temporal doubts of His people, 'the foundation of the Lord standeth sure, having this seal, the Lord knoweth them that are His.'[8]

His abiding sense of divine sovereignty so engulfed his soul that he could not pass a day of diary entry without some energetic burst of adoration of divine wisdom and mercy. His ability to apply these truths so gracefully and naturally in his preaching came from his having constantly celebrated this reality in transparently loving terms from the first day of his new life in Christ. The

---

7. Ibid., p. 134.
8. Ibid., To his Father, 6 April 1850.

pulpit discourse and peroration that so transfixed his auditory emerged out of the depth of his personal persuasion of God's saving operation in his own case. 'The Lord has visited me from on high. Rejoice, O my soul, leap for joy, renew thy strength; run, run, in the name of the Lord!' he wrote on 19 May 1850. 'Free grace, sovereign love, eternal security are my safeguards; what shall keep me from consecrating all to Thee, even to the last drop of my blood?' he asked on 25 May. He confided to his diary on 29 May: 'How happy am I to be one of His chosen, His elect, in whom His soul delighteth. ... Make me Thy faithful servant, O my God; may I honour Thee in my day and generation, and be consecrated for ever to Thy service!'

The next to the last dated entry was on 19 June, his birthday, when he noted that his true life began only at his conversion:

> My birthday. Sixteen years have I lived upon this earth, and yet I am only six months old! I am very young in grace. Yet how much time have I wasted, dead in trespasses and sins, without life, without God, in the world! What a mercy that I did not perish in my sin! How glorious is my calling, how exalted my election, born of the Lord – regenerate! Help me more than ever to walk worthily, as becomes a saint![9]

In an undated addition, near the end of the manuscript, Spurgeon penned a prayer that distilled the nature of his pastoral ministry, soon to be inaugurated: 'May I know the joy and have the faith of God's elect; may I rejoice in free sovereign grace, saving me from the guilt and power of sin! Grace is a glorious theme, above the loftiest flights of the most soaring angel, or the most exalted conceptions of one of the joint-heirs with Jesus.' He closed the paragraph with a statement of the confidence that sustained him in the fulfillment of his closing request: 'All power is God's, and all is engaged to protect and preserve me. Let me have my daily grace, peace and comfort, zeal and love, give me some work, and give me strength to do it to Thy glory!'

---

9. Ibid., p. 142.

The Substance of the Preacher's Work

From the First Day

Spurgeon confirmed that this truth dwelt alongside him from the first day of his ministry and was his boon companion when he looked back over twenty-five years as pastor in London. 'The gospel of the grace of God has been continually preached from the first day until now,' he remarked; 'the same gospel, we trust accompanied with growing experience and appreciation and knowledge, but not another gospel, nor even another form of the same gospel.'[10] This was no exaggeration, for in the first volume of sermons issued from the pulpit of New Park Street, Spurgeon said, 'I love to proclaim these strong old doctrines which are called by nickname, Calvinism, but which are surely and verily the revealed truth of God as it is in Christ Jesus!'[11]

His stance on these truths was shocking to the polite and elegant Victorian pulpit and the most prestigious religious periodicals of the day. He felt their disdain but did not flinch in his determination to preach what was clearly true in Scripture and had been embraced in that pristine purity in the confessions that preserved the beliefs of the past. When he cited these, he confessed: 'I have only used them as a kind of confirmation to your faith, to show you that while I may be railed upon as a heretic and as a hyper-Calvinist, after all I am backed up by antiquity! All the past stands by me. I do not care for the present. Give me the past and I will hope for the future. Let the present rise up in my teeth, I will not care.' Even if 'a host of the churches of London may have forsaken the great cardinal doctrines of God', still he would persevere in 'an unflinching maintenance of the sovereignty of our God'.[12]

On 11 February 1855, Spurgeon did much to promote the culture of shock and resistance around his ministry when he preached on 'Christ Crucified'. This was the first Sunday in Exeter Hall,

---

10. Ernest LeVos, p. 8.
11. SS 2:69; NPSP 1:41.
12. SS 2:70.

when the church met there from 11 February through 27 May, during renovation of the New Park Street building. Papers reported that 'the Strand was blocked up by crowds who gathered to hear a young man in Exeter Hall'. At the same time, journals opined in 'no very flattering character'. Fabricated stories and 'the most cruel lies' accompanied caricatures that rapidly appeared in print sellers' windows. These increased the opposition on the one hand and swelled the crowds on the other.

His sermon that day, heard by more Londoners from more spheres of influence and more areas of population than had heard him before, gave cartoonists their nickname of 'Brimstone' for the twenty-one-year-old phenomenon. After he ridiculed the failures of worldly wisdom, philosophy, and religious contrivances to find a way for true worship and forgiveness of sins, he proposed 'Christ and Him crucified' as God's wisdom confuting all other ways in the history of human thought and religion. This had a specifically Calvinistic bent for Spurgeon:

> And I have my own private opinion that there is no such a thing as preaching Christ, and Him crucified, unless you preach what now-a-days is called Calvinism. I have my own ideas, and those I always state boldly. It is a nickname to call it Calvinism; Calvinism is the gospel and nothing else! I do not believe we can preach the gospel if we do not preach justification by faith, without works; nor unless we preach the sovereignty of God in His dispensation of grace. Nor unless we exalt the electing, unchangeable, eternal, immutable, conquering love of Jehovah! Nor do I think we can preach the gospel unless we base it upon the peculiar redemption which Christ made for His elect and chosen people. Nor can I comprehend a gospel which lets saints fall away after they are called and suffers the children of God to be burned in the fires of damnation after having believed! Such a gospel I abhor! The gospel of the Bible is not such a gospel as that. We preach Christ and Him crucified in a different fashion and to all gainsayers we reply, 'We have not so learned Christ.'[13]

---

13. SS 2:88, 89.

Criticism did not temper his convictions or his boldness in proclaiming them. As a manifestation of this conviction, in September 1855, Spurgeon preached from 2 Thessalonians 2:13, 14. The sermon was entitled 'Unconditional Election'. He began the discourse: 'If there were no other text in the sacred Word except this one, I think we would all be bound to receive and acknowledge the truthfulness of the great and glorious doctrine of God's ancient choice of His family. But there seems to be an inveterate prejudice in the human mind against this doctrine – and although most other doctrines will be received by professing Christians, some with caution, others with pleasure – this one seems to be most frequently disregarded and discarded!' He proceeded to describe unconditional election as undeniably truthful, absolute, eternal, and personal. The Bible words behind the exposition were 'God has from the beginning chosen you to salvation through sanctification of the Spirit and belief of the truth' (KJV).

Spurgeon explained that God, in electing His people to salvation, has no regard to any virtue or foreseen faith in them, for faith and virtue are products, not causes of election. God looks only to His own will, a will that is coeternal with His very being and thus places His particular displays of electing redemptive love on specific individuals within His affections and wisdom as a matter of constant, ever-existing consent. It is unto holiness, so none but those pressing toward holiness are elect. It keeps us for Jesus Christ, so none but those who yearn to know and be like Jesus are elect. It is humbling, infinitely so, therefore none of the arrogant, prideful, and self-sufficient are elect. It rescues from sin, ignorance, rebellion, and corruption, so it is the only hope of fallen sinners. Unconditional election, in such a view, should not generate opposition, but gratitude; should not plunge to despair, but should stir hope.

On 6 April 1856, Spurgeon continued his regular exposition of the doctrines of grace with a sermon entitled 'Effectual Calling'. He began this discourse, in which he did an extended theological analysis of the salvation of Zacchaeus, by consenting that most of those who heard him were 'well instructed in the doctrines of the everlasting gospel'. Conversations with young converts, however, reminded him 'how absolutely necessary it is to repeat our former lessons and repeatedly assert and prove over and over again those doctrines which lie at the basis of our holy religion'. This truth Spurgeon called 'this great starting point of God in the heart – the effectual calling of men by the Holy Spirit.'

Two weeks later, on 20 April 1856, he preached on 'Perseverance of the Saints'. Taking Hebrews 6:4-6 as his sermonic passage, he disagreed with both John Gill and John Owen in saying that those described in the passage were true believers. The text's teaching the 'impossibility' of being renewed to repentance after 'falling away', not only demolished any Arminian understanding of apostasy and regained salvation but was the calculated means of preserving the elect ever from such falling away.

In 'A Visit to Calvary', preached in 1856, the young pastor preached on Pilate's words 'Behold, the Man,' with a quite different motive from the Roman Procurator. He wanted to point out the glory of Christ as seen in His sufferings. In beholding Christ, one will see the *the inflexibility of divine justice*. God's justice as presented through the Law utters an inflexible and unchangeable curse on its transgressors. God by no means will spare the guilty. Yet some preach an atonement that shies away from substitution and wrath. 'We believe,' Spurgeon countered, 'that God is so just, that every sinner must be punished, that every crime must inevitably have its doom.' Consequently, in Christ's atonement, if it is the source of forgiveness, 'all the punishment which God's people ought to have endured was laid upon the head of Christ.' The crucifixion of the Beloved demonstrates that God's justice is 'unchanging, unvarying,' and that 'the punishment for that guilt was actually and absolutely borne by Christ'. Since sin has been punished absolutely in Christ, it 'ceases to be punishable in the persons of those for whom Christ died'.[14] George

---

14. SS 2:332, 333.

Herbert (1593–1633), Spurgeon's favorite poet, was quoted as having captured the intensity of the moral transaction:

> Who would know Sin, let him repair
> Unto Mount Olivet; there shall he see
> A man, so wrung with pains, that all his hair,
> His skin, his garments, bloody be.
> Sin is that Press and Vice, which forceth pain
> To hunt his cruel food through every vein.

In 1857 the third volume of Spurgeon's American edition of his sermons was published by Sheldon, Blakeman, and Company. In the preface to that volume, Spurgeon noted that his sermons had been used greatly of the Lord to bring 'forth fruits meet for repentance' but had some cautions about the overall state of preaching. His experience of opposition, even outrage, had increased the caution with which he evaluated the English pulpit. 'Let a brother beseech you,' he admonished his American brethren, 'to maintain the faith, once delivered to the saints, whole and inviolable.' He saw that England had been blessed 'with some blessed gleams of sunshine', but some who discerned what was happening beneath the surface 'are led frequently to tremble for the ark of the Lord'. Why? 'Arminianism secretly lurks among us. Our ministers prune the truth, and conceal the great distinguishing doctrines of grace, in a manner much to be lamented.' On the other hand, 'Antinomianism, through its perversions of the truth, has done much to check the advance of sound opinions, and has made many good men cautious of being too high, that they have run into the opposite extremes of error.'[15] He was determined, however, that neither the Arminian nor the antinomian would win the day.

And Every Day thereafter

An example of Spurgeon's continuing focus on the details of the Doctrines of Grace, may be seen in his argument presented in

---

15. SS 3, preface vi.

a sermon from March 1859 on 'Predestination and Calling'. He carefully delineated between the universal, or general, call and the effectual call. The universal call comes to all who hear the gospel while the effectual call comes only to those who have been predestinated to such in the eternal covenant of redemption, the 'great book of God's decrees'. This matter of eternal concern puts all temporal matters to naught in its weightiness. May one peer into the book and see whether his name is there or not? No, God has not revealed the names this side of eternity, but only the character of those whose names are in the book. The character can be distilled into the effects of one's calling. The universal call goes out to the multitude. Those who reject it are 'without excuse in the rejection'. Even this call 'has in it such authority that the man, who will not obey it, shall be without excuse in the day of judgment.'[16] In 1862, preaching on election, Spurgeon reinforced this truth in saying, 'You may rest perfectly sure that falling back on the doctrine of election in order to exonerate you from what God commands you to perform is but a pitiful pretence.'[17] Spurgeon's strong commitment to the doctrines of grace did not for one moment move him to deny the obligations of all persons to every spiritual duty. As surely as it is the duty of all persons to love God with all the heart, mind, and soul, so it is the duty of each sinner to repent and believe the gospel. When Jesus and the apostles called on the crowds to follow Christ, or repent of sin, or believe the gospel, they called them 'to none other than a saving faith, and it is frivolous to say otherwise.' Though faith is a special gift to the elect only, it remains, nevertheless, the 'duty of all men'. All men must believe the truth and all men must love and trust the only One who is worthy of both. A man's spiritual inability is a perversity within his nature and constitutes no excuse for dereliction of duty. 'It is altogether an error to imagine,' Spurgeon argued, 'that the measure of the sinner's

16. NPSP 5: Sermon 241.
17. SEE 7:12.

moral ability is the measure of his duty.' No matter how bad men may be, their badness does not render Christ's command to repent irrelevant to them, for their inability to follow and close with the command arises precisely from their badness, defines it, and even aggravates it.[18]

But the sinner's spiritual deadness, expressed in his active rebellion against God, requires that something endowed with greater transformative power than that of words to the ears and mind must operate – 'not only in word, but also in power and in the Holy Spirit and with full conviction' (1 Thess. 1:5). This unrelenting, omnivictorious power is denominated effectual calling. This calling comes in accordance with submission to the truth and so engages the mind; it appeals to motivation and so engages the will. But both mind and will, both the noetic and affective elements of human nature, are pressed down under moral turpitude and can only be released by the creative, transformative operation of a personal force of holiness. Only so can the holy claims of the gospel be embraced by a fallen child of Adam.

The effects of such a calling, therefore, give the evidence of one's predestination. God has so filled Scripture with its characteristics that the called and, therefore, predestinated may know their status with certainty. Using several Scripture references that give traits of this calling, Spurgeon gave its contours: holy, heavenly, high, producing repentance, fellowship with Christ, granting freedom from sin and guilt, prompting escape from darkness toward the light. These are the marks of calling and may bring a person to rejoice in his election. 'Oh, what a glorious doctrine is that of election, when a man can see himself to be elect!' Many hate the doctrine of election. If, however, they also revolt at the idea of holiness and blamelessness they should be satisfied to be among the non-elect, for they will never be forced to become what they have no desire to become. If its creation of distinctives offends them, then its traits of true holiness

---

18. MTP 17: 'Faith and Regeneration.'

also offend them. 'One of the reasons why many men kick against it is this,' Spurgeon surmised, 'they are afraid it hurts them. I never yet knew a man who had a reason to believe that he was chosen of God, who hated the doctrine of election!'[19]

Again in 1859, Spurgeon focused on the certainty of salvation elicited by a right understanding of the covenant of redemption. In 'The Blood of the Everlasting Covenant', Spurgeon called attention to 'the high contracting Parties between whom it was made'.[20] In its full scriptural light, the covenant reflects a perfect eternal agreement resident within the Godhead. It has always been operative 'mutually between the Three Divine Persons of the adorable Trinity'. It was not 'made mutually between God and man', but 'Christ stood in the Covenant as man's Representative'. In that sense, man can be seen as a partner in the covenant, but not any individual personally, but only as incorporated in Christ as representative. 'It was a Covenant between God with Christ and through Christ indirectly with all the blood-bought seed who were loved of Christ from before the foundation of the world!' This noble and glorious thought, this transcendent poetry of grace and redemption, constituted 'that old Calvinistic Doctrine which we teach'. It affirmed that long before stars or moons or light itself or any creative utterance issued from the triune God, 'He had entered into solemn council with Himself, with His Son and with His Spirit and had in that council decreed, determined, proposed and predestinated the Salvation of His people!' This salvation would be arranged through settled means consistent with the eternal purpose and immutable character of God.

In contemplation of such transfixing reality, Spurgeon struggled to find barriers to his desire to be party to the divine conversation. 'My soul flies back, now, winged by imagination and by faith and looks into that mysterious council chamber,' he admitted. 'By faith' – he loaded the vision with biblical safeguards – 'I behold the

---

19. NPSP 5: Sermon 241.
20. NPSP 5: Sermon 277.

Father pledging Himself to the Son and the Son pledging Himself to the Father, while the Spirit gives His pledge to both and thus that Divine Compact, long to be hidden in darkness, is completed and settled.' He was unwaveringly aware that his reconstruction of human relations and interactions was replete with limitations. He set it forth merely as an analogous relation in time to the perfections of the immanent, intrinsic, eternal agreement within the divine will as held fittingly by each person of the Trinity. Nevertheless, reaching as highly and as clearly into the covenantal agreement which led to his salvation challenged his mind and ravished his heart – 'the Covenant which in these latter days has been read in the light of Heaven and has become the joy and hope and boast of all the saints!'

In 1862, we find Spurgeon still enamored with the covenantal arrangement in eternity of the three persons of God for the salvation of all the persons whom He would save. In 'Threefold Sanctification', Spurgeon asked his congregation to mark 'the union of the Three Divine Persons in all their gracious acts!' Heightening the singularity of this work, Spurgeon wanted to emphasize that, 'although we rejoice to recognize the Trinity, yet it is ever most distinctly a Trinity in Unity.' Like the cry given to Israel of old, 'The LORD our God is one LORD.' The Christian must avoid making preferences in the Trinity, such as preferring the power of the Spirit or of the condescending love of Jesus or of some aspect of the Father's gracious operations as if there were competition or shades of quality in the work of any of the divine persons. Most frequently one may be tempted to 'think of Christ as if He were the embodiment of everything that is lovely and gracious, while the Father they regard as severely just, but destitute of kindness.' At other times one might 'magnify the Decree of the Father, or the Atonement of the Son, so as to depreciate the work of the Spirit.'[21]

In a profoundly worshipful and practical application of the doctrine of *circumincessio*, Spurgeon reminded the congregation

---

21. MTP 8:434: 'Threefold Sanctification.'

that in 'deeds of Divine Grace none of the Persons of the Trinity act apart from the rest. They are as united in their deeds as in their Essence!' Their love towards the chosen has no distinction in quality or quantity; the consequent actions of such purpose of love is without division in its energy and effectuality and purpose. For example, in the work of sanctification, one may speak of sanctification as the 'work of the Spirit, yet, we must take heed that we do not view it as if the Father and the Son had no part in it!' We correctly speak of sanctification 'as the work of the Father, of the Spirit, and of the Son. Still does Jehovah, the triune God, who said, "Let Us make man in Our Own image, after Our likeness," speak.' Even so in sanctification, 'We are "His workmanship, created in Christ Jesus unto good works, which God has before ordained that we should walk in them".'

A True Calvinist

Without any danger of diminishing the importance of the divine unity, Spurgeon looked at the work of the Son as the center-piece of this eternal covenant. His was the consent to bear the punishments due to the people predestined to be redeemed by the terms of the covenant. In his discussion of the relation between an atonement precisely designed for the elect and the universal call and duty to believe, Spurgeon avoided the hyper-Calvinist error. They defined faith as consisting of the confidence that Christ died for them in particular. Spurgeon, to the contrary, stated that faith 'is not the assurance that Jesus died for me'. He took issue even with the line of the hymn 'Just As I Am' that states 'Just as I am, without one plea, but that thy blood was shed for me.' That is powerful confidence for the saints but an unnecessary, and faulty, appeal to be made to the sinner.

Hyper-Calvinists shared a common error with Arminians in asserting that one could not have faith unless he had assurance that Christ had died for him. If faith is that precise persuasion that Christ has died for me in particular (and it must be true if Christ has died for all men without exception), then all believers in a universal atonement have such a persuasion. 'On such a theory every believer in a universal atonement would necessarily be born of God, which is very far from being the case.' Spurgeon feared that thousands of people believe that Jesus died for them 'who are not born of God, but rather are hardened in their sin by their groundless hopes of mercy.' Sinners come into saving faith only when they come under the 'general character' of sinners and in reliance on the universal proposition that all who trust in Him as the effectual Savior of sinners will find acceptance.

They come apart from any prior guarantee that Christ has died for them in particular, but only on the persuasion of their desperate need, that He only can meet that need if He grants such mercy, and that the promise of forgiveness is for those who so come. The only warrant for certainty is the promise to coming sinners of not being pushed away. 'In my first coming to Jesus I can have no knowledge of any personal and special interest in the blood of Jesus.' But since Jesus is the only propitiation for sins, one trusts in that propitiation under His invitation, yea command, to come. In coming, the sinner lays hands on Jesus 'desiring to receive the benefit of His substitutionary death'. A yearning, utterly dependent, glance at the Savior, a desperate and hopeful touching of the raveling of His robe, embodies the faith of God's elect. One discovers from such a look or such a touch that he or she is the 'object of His special love', and the subject of Spirit-generated saving faith.[22]

From his earliest days in London, Spurgeon had to live with the attacks and misrepresentations of the hyper-Calvinists. He had no intention of allowing their shared passion for the doctrines of grace drive him to their doctrinal deformity; nor did he allow his resistance to their criticism press him into any less clarity and passion about divine sovereignty in every aspect of redemption. He knew of some people 'of a certain class' who delight in God's words

---

22. MTP 17:979: 'Faith and Regeneration.'

about the doctrines of grace and the freeness of redemption, but they 'will be as angry as though you had touched them with a hot iron if you should bring a precept anywhere near them.' Words of duty 'sting them like a whip' and reminders that salvation includes sanctification and holiness as well as justification bring about the charge of 'Arminianism' and the opprobrious characterization of being 'duty-faith' men.[23]

Spurgeon understood both the theology and the temperament of the hyper-Calvinists. He found some to be genuinely pious and spiritual men, but, as he saw things, misled about the fullness of divine revelation. They were zealous for many of the right things – so much so that Spurgeon believed that a couple of score of hyper-Calvinists among the Anglicans could do the established church good – but truncated in their grasp of the relation between sovereignty and means, grace and duty, depravity and culpability. They rang five bells, or played five strings, rather heartily but failed to bring in the entire orchestra which made the bells fit with beauty and symmetry. Rather than creating a trust in the promises of Scripture and driving sinners to believe God in His Word, they taught them to expect a special revelation from heaven of their election and of Christ's death for them in particular. They created both despair and presumption.

Prolonged in Conviction, Undiminished in Certainty

Though ignored by some and reprehended by others, Spurgeon wanted no diminution of emphasis on the invincible purpose of God. In a sermon on the Lord's Supper, not published until 1908, Spurgeon scoffed at the supposedly enlightened nineteenth century and its facile dismissal of orthodox confessional doctrine. 'No,' he responded, 'That truth of God which of old was mighty through God to the pulling down of strongholds, is still mighty, and we will maintain it to the death! The church needs the doctrines of grace today as much as

---

23. SEE 15:173.

when Paul, or Augustine, or Calvin preached them! The church needs justification by faith, the substitutionary atonement, regeneration and divine sovereignty to be preached from her pulpits as much as in days of yore! And by God's grace she shall have them, too!'[24]

Among the several uses of the concept of 'word of God' that Spurgeon noted, one was the 'word of His purpose'. All that God has purposed will come to pass. Preeminent in all things that God has purposed is the manifestation of 'all His attributes in the salvation of His people'. Though ministers seldom preach about God's predestination of an elect unto eternal life, they are not companions of the Apostle Paul in their fearful or faithless hesitation. As for Spurgeon, he joined Paul and the saints of old in proclaiming that 'though before conversion they plunge into sin; ay, and though during their conversion they resist the Spirit of God, ay, and though after conversion they go astray like lost sheep, yet shall the wondrous power of sovereign grace be more than a match for the waywardness of nature, and the will of God shall sweetly lead in divine captivity the will of man, and though the man resolveth on his own destruction, God, who ordaineth salvation, shall accomplish His own purpose, earth and hell notwithstanding.'[25]

In 1858, at the Surrey Garden Music Hall, Spurgeon preached on particular redemption from the Lukan text, 'The Son of Man has come to seek and to save that which was lost.' In his introductory words he argued that the concept of general redemption was 'that Jesus Christ has shed His blood for every man and that the intention of Christ in His death was the salvation of men considered as a whole.' If such were the case, then 'Christ's intention would be frustrated in a measure'. Spurgeon himself opted for 'particular redemption or limited atonement'. While he acknowledged that 'the blood of Christ was of an infinite value', yet 'the intention of the death of Christ never was the salvation of all men'. If that

24. SEE 10:315. Also found in MTP 54 under the title 'Christ and His Table-Companions'.
25. SEE 15:188.

were the case, 'we hold that all men would have been saved!' No, the intention of Christ's death is commensurate with its effect. He determined to preach, therefore, 'a self-evident truth' that 'whatever was the intention of Jesus Christ in coming into the world – that intention most certainly shall be fulfilled.'

In 1875, Spurgeon preached a series on Jesus: as Substitute, as the Stumbling Stone, and as the Delight of Heaven. In Jesus as the Delight of Heaven, Spurgeon expanded on the testimony that Christ alone was worthy to break the sevenfold seal of the book, for He had died and had redeemed men to God. In this exposition Spurgeon noted that 'He must render recompense to incensed Justice and injured Holiness – and that He did upon the bloody tree!' Spurgeon interpreted this as absolute payment for every transgression of the elect even under the cloud of being accused of a commercial view of the atonement. 'Oh, you hold the commercial theory, do you?' Spurgeon countered that he used commercial language precisely in line with Scripture language. 'You may well assert that there is nothing commercial about your system,' Spurgeon objected, 'for the commercial value of a counterfeit farthing would be too much to pay for the atonement in which you believe.' He believed that 'Christ literally took the sin of His people, and for them endured the Wrath of God, giving to Justice *quid pro quo* for all that was due to it.' He asserted a literal, positive, actual substitution as necessary to bring us to God. 'No other atonement,' Spurgeon announced, 'is worth the breath used in preaching of it! It will neither give comfort to the conscience nor Glory to God.' The so-called, but misnomered, General Redemption 'is not worth anything to anybody, for of itself it secures to no one a place in Heaven.' The actual redemption of His elect is what was aimed at and was accomplished in Christ's substitution for sinners.[26]

A rare caveat came in 1867 when Spurgeon preached on 'The Great Mystery of Godliness'. Dealing with the confession of 1 Timothy

---

26. MTP 21:1225: 'Jesus, the Delight of Heaven.'

3:16, Spurgeon said that the text was 'no mere exhibition of doctrine'. Affirming that he believed 'most firmly in the doctrines called Calvinistic', he held them to be 'very fraught with comfort to God's people'. He would take issue, he noted, with some who contended that 'preaching of these is the whole of the preaching of the gospel'. The doctrines of election, final perseverance and others go to make up a complete ministry, yet he pointed out that 'some who have denied those truths, to our great grief, have nevertheless been gospel preachers for all that, and God has saved souls by their ministry.' The death, burial, and resurrection of Christ as urged by Paul in 1 Corinthians 15 – the facts of Christ's historic redemptive work and the promise of life through Him – 'these are the faith of the gospel.'[27]

In 1891, in the last sermon Spurgeon preached in the Tabernacle, he still proclaimed the blessings of the covenant as they streamed forth to the people of God by free grace. Pointing to how David shared the spoil of victory over the Amalekites with all, even with the two hundred that could not go to the fight but stayed with the baggage:

> Look upon every blessing as a gift and you will not think any shut out from it, not even yourself! The gift of God is eternal life – why should you not have it? Deny not to anyone of your Brothers and Sisters any comfort of the Covenant of Grace. Think not of any man, 'He ought not to have so much joy.' It is all of Free Grace and if Free Grace rules the hour, the least may have it as well as the greatest! If it is all of Free Grace, then, my poor struggling Brother, who can hardly feel assured that you are saved, yet if you are a Believer, you may claim every blessing of the Lord's gracious Covenant! God freely gives to you as well as to me the provisions of His love – therefore let us be glad and not judge ourselves after the manner of the law of condemnation![28]

---

27. SEE 3:18, 19.
28. MTP 37:2208: 'The Statute of David for the Sharing of the Spoil.'

3

'HE DOES NOT BLAME ME FOR BEING A BAPTIST'

A Personal Persuasion

Spurgeon was reared under the powerful influence of two devoted Congregational ministers, his father and his grandfather, who practiced and argued doctrinally for infant baptism. Spurgeon, early in his ministry at New Park Street, explained that Christians must come to their convictions on this issue by means of Scripture alone, and not from the religious persuasion of their parents. He argued that the Baptist formulation of Christian commitment was the purest biblical expression. He asked, 'Did any of you ever sit down to see which was the purest religion?' Should they answer that they never took the trouble, but only went 'just where our father and mother went', he chided, 'Ah, that is a profound reason, indeed!' He did not think that sensible people went 'where other people pulled you, but went of your own selves.'

To illustrate the necessity of personal conviction on this point, Spurgeon continued: 'I love my parents above all that breathe and the very thought that they believed a thing to be true, helps me to think it is correct.' He had not followed them, however; but, as he stated, 'I belong to a different denomination – and I thank God I do.'[1] The tenderness and gratitude with which he regarded

---

1. SS 1:35, 36.

his sire and grand-sire and his devoted mother and grandmother predisposed him toward open communion in his eventual practice at the Lord's Table, but again his own personal conviction would not allow him to receive communion until he had been baptized. Here is the story.

An Early Impression Becomes a Strong Conviction

Until Spurgeon was fourteen years old, he had not even heard of a people called 'Baptists'. When he did hear of them, the report was not favorable. Whether his parents believed that Baptists were bad people, he could not remember, but he recalled: 'I certainly did think so; and I cannot help feeling that, somewhere or other I must have heard some calumnies against them, or else how should I have that opinion?'[2]

In spite of this mysteriously implanted impression about Baptists, Spurgeon also had seeds of doubt about infant baptism planted in his conscience. He recalled seeing a baby baptized within an hour of its death and recalled the minister telling the parents, 'What a mercy the child was baptized! What a consolation it must be!' Adding to the impression was the fact that this sense of safety in baptism was expressed by an 'Independent minister', supposedly immune to the superstitions of the Anglican Prayer Book concerning the saving power of baptism. This attempt at pastoral assurance was given to 'an independent family'.[3] On another occasion he heard of a minister who, against the father's will, sprinkled an unruly child. While making a disturbance in the manse, the child was apprehended by the minister, and, with the approval of his mother, the minister sprinkled the child so that he would live no longer like a heathen. Spurgeon summarized: 'So the conjuration was performed, and the little boy was put into the Paedo-Baptist covenant.' Having been forced to come, he went his way rejoicing that the solemn event was over.

---

2. *Autobiography*, 1:45.
3. Ibid., 1:45.

These events clearly were anomalous, but their exceptional nature established pause in Spurgeon's mind about the authority for either unconscious or unwilling submission to the ordinance of baptism. Spurgeon credits an Anglican teacher with sealing his convictions about scriptural baptism. In the school at Maidstone, the teacher, while working through the Anglican catechism, learned that Spurgeon's father and grandfather were independent ministers and that Spurgeon had been baptized by his grandfather, in a parlor, as an infant, and without sponsors. Since his grandfather performed the ceremony, it did not bother Spurgeon since 'all infants ought to be baptized', so he had learned. Seizing the opportunity to pick what he thought was low-hanging fruit, the clergyman-teacher sought to convince Spurgeon that his baptism was false but that of the Church of England was true. Spurgeon concluded that neither his nor the Anglican's doctrine was consistent with the New Testament.

Announcing the contest to Spurgeon, his teacher showed that the New Testament records that only those that profess faith may be baptized – 'Does not the Prayer Book say that faith and repentance are necessary before baptism?' The Congregationalists, however, baptize infants without sponsors to profess their faith vicariously. To the contrary, Anglicans baptize infants with sponsors who pledge their faith for them and also denounce the devil and all his ways. The obvious conclusion to the mind of the minster was that Congregational baptism was wrong, because done in the absence of faith, and Anglican baptism was right, for it was performed on the basis of a sponsor professing the infant's faith. After a week of searching the New Testament, Spurgeon concluded that the teacher was partly right but still wrong. He could not find baptism without repentance and faith, but neither could he find sponsors for another's faith. Spurgeon responded, therefore, at their next discussion that having sponsors did not seem to prove the point of the New Testament idea of faith. He had already been baptized once wrongly, and he would 'wait next time till I am fit for it'. At that moment he resolved 'that if ever Divine grace should work a change in me, I would be baptized.'[4]

In January 1850, only a few weeks after his conversion, he wrote his mother effusively rejoicing in the love of Jesus, the beauty and power of the Bible, the effectual operations of the Spirit, the dread of any sin against the saving grace of God, and a remembrance of 'the horrible pit and hole from which I have been digged'. He also stated his conviction that 'it is a part of duty openly to profess Him'. He added that he firmly believed that 'baptism is the command of Christ', and that he would not 'feel quite comfortable if I do not receive it'.[5]

In February he wrote his mother: 'Conscience has convinced me that it is a duty to be buried with Christ in baptism, although I am sure it constitutes no part of salvation. I am very glad that you have no objections to my doing so.' In April he wrote his father telling him of his hesitancy to sit at the Lord's Table until he was baptized. For those not so convinced, he felt no resistance to their being partakers, but 'if I were to do so, I conceive it would be to tumble over the wall, since I feel persuaded it is Christ's appointed way of professing Him. I am sure this is the only view which I have of baptism.' He wanted neither to 'tumble over the wall', as some without a biblically mandated profession did in Bunyan's immortal allegory, nor did he want to advocate any saving power in the ordinance itself. In his last paragraph, Spurgeon reminded his father: 'As Mr Cantlow's baptizing season will come round this month, I have humbly to beg your consent, as I will not act against your will, and should very much like to commune next month.' He expressed confidence in his father's permission, his joy in their union in Christ in spite of their difference in 'forms and ceremonies'.[6]

Later, Charles wrote an urgent letter to his mother soliciting her intervention in case his father was hardening against his son's

4. Ibid., 1:34, 35.
5. Murray, *Letters,* p. 20.
6. Murray, *Letters,* pp. 22-25. *Autobiography,* 1:112-16.

wishes. 'I have every morning looked for a letter from Father,' making no attempt to hide his anxiety over this; 'I long for an answer; it is now a month since I have had one from him. Do, if you please, send me either permission or refusal to be baptized; I have been kept in painful suspense.'[7]

Buried With Christ in Baptism

Permission came and on 24 April 1850 Spurgeon wrote in his diary, 'I am to do as I please about baptism.' Evidently, his father placed all the responsibility for the act on Spurgeon's conscience, and Spurgeon reflected, 'Never do I lose anything by zeal for the truth.' Dubious about his son's conviction, the elder Spurgeon made the decision for Spurgeon as difficult as he could without forbidding him. 'In truth,' Spurgeon sighed, after receiving a letter from his father, 'he is rather hard upon me. When I followed my conscience, and did not presumptuously break through the fences of the Lord about his church, I might have expected this.' Given the way forward to be his own pilgrimage, Spurgeon said, 'My business is to follow my Saviour and not to pick out smooth paths for myself.' The young convert knew that, in spite of opposition implied, his walk in the truth would be a testimony to the faithfulness of God and would embolden him against reproach and against enemies that sought to make him quail with terror. His father's chief fear was that Charles would 'trust to baptism'. Spurgeon himself hated such a thought and proclaimed with certainty that even if he could 'from this day be as holy as God Himself, yet I could not atone for past sin.' Two days before his baptism, Spurgeon confided to his diary: 'The time of my baptism approaches. May I die to the world, and live alone for Thee!' The peril of fear and resistance, however, still loomed before his soul as he prayed: 'I would serve Thee, O Lord, but I feel a weight, a law working against this law, and holding me in partial bondage; let Thy grace break every fetter that withholds my heart from Thee!'[8]

---

7. *Autobiography*, 1:116.
8. Ibid., 1:129-31.

On 3 May 1850, his mother's birthday, he walked eight miles with Mr Cantlow to Isleham Ferry on the river Lark. The river divides Suffolk from Cambridgeshire. The first baptism recorded at Isleham came in 1798 when Andrew Fuller baptized a father and his son and three others. Spurgeon recorded the details of his own baptism: 'Started with Mr Cantlow at eleven, reached Isleham at one o'clock. In the afternoon, I was privileged to follow my Lord, and to be buried with Him in baptism. Blest pool! Sweet emblem of my death to all the world! May I, henceforward, live alone for Jesus! Accept my body and soul as a poor sacrifice, tie me unto Thee; in Thy strength I now devote myself to Thy service forever; never may I shrink from owning Thy name!'[9]

The day of Spurgeon's baptism was cool and the gusty wind made the elements of baptism startling and bracing. One of the aids had started a peat fire for warmth and onlookers stood in boats and on the ferry and on the bank. Spurgeon described the thoroughly solemn joy he experienced:

> The wind blew down the river with a cutting blast, as my turn came to wade into the flood, but after I had walked a few steps, and noted the people on the ferry-boats, and in boats, and on either shore, I felt as if Heaven, and earth, and hell, might all gaze upon me, for I was not ashamed, there and then, to own myself a follower of the Lamb. My timidity was washed away; it floated down the river into the sea, and must have been devoured by the fishes, for I have never felt anything of the kind since. Baptism also loosed my tongue, and from that day it has never been quiet. I lost a thousand fears in that River Lark, and found that 'in keeping his commandments there is great reward.'[10]

In June 1850, Spurgeon reported to his mother that his grandfather 'does not blame me for being a Baptist'. He did hope, however, that he would not be 'one of the tight-laced, strict-communion sort'. He expressed his agreement with his grandfather on that point: 'I

---

9. Ibid., 1:135.
10. *Autobiography*, 1:149, 150.

certainly think we ought to forget such things in others when we come to the Lord's table. I can, and hope I shall be charitable to unbaptized Christians, though I think they are mistaken.' When compared to agreement on vital gospel issues, Spurgeon did not view this difference as 'a great matter'. Each must follow his conscience in this and spend time more profitably 'in talking upon vital godliness than in disputing about forms'.[11]

In 1861 at the opening of the Metropolitan Tabernacle, John Spurgeon presided. In comments he made early in the program he rejoiced that 'there is so much harmony between us, even though we may differ, perhaps, in some points of view.' As he pointed to the water in the baptistry, he continued, 'I do not see clearly into this water before me, but if I did I would go down and be baptized at once.' He then encouraged all those present who felt that the command of believers' baptism was true, 'It is your sin if you live another week without it.' They should not burden their conscience or put shadows on their relation with God by the neglect of something felt to be a 'bounden duty'.[12]

The story has been told often, and as true it bears repeating. Spurgeon's mother remarked that when she prayed the Lord would convert her eldest son, she did not request that he would become a Baptist. Young Spurgeon replied, 'Ah, mother! The Lord has answered your prayer with His usual bounty, and given you exceeding abundantly above what you asked or thought.'[13]

A Baptist Preacher

Church Membership

Spurgeon's conviction that only regenerate people should be received as church members pressed him into Baptist life. In 1874 Spurgeon preached from Acts 2:47 on 'Additions to the Church' and invited all who were 'thinking about joining the church to search and

---

11. Murray, *Letters* p. 28. *Autobiography*, 1:119.
12. MTP 7:380: 'Meeting of Our Own Church.'
13. *Autobiography*, 1:45.

see whether you are such as the Lord would add to a church'. He looked for such as had been wounded and healed by the Lord and who trusted in the Lord as their righteousness. He looked for those made new by the Spirit and clearly were subjects of divine agency. 'Oh, dear friends who love the Lord,' Spurgeon implored, 'join in earnest prayer that the Lord would add to the church daily the saved ones, for we long for such!' Looking at the text, Spurgeon insisted, 'Saved persons were added to the church – and only such are fit to be added!' He had no authority to receive any but such as the Lord Himself added, only believers. 'The proper persons to be added to the visible church of Christ are those who believe to the salvation of their souls.' These believers have a saving work continuing, delivered from the reign of sin, kept by divine power to be 'presented at last, spotless before the presence of God with exceeding joy!' The door to the church is 'wide open to all who are saved, however little their faith may be', for the church has no prerogative 'to exclude any of the saved because their knowledge or experience is not that of advanced believers'. Babes are of the family and should be received, for church membership is 'not a certificate of advanced Christianity'. No limbs may be tied to the tree; eventually they wither and will destroy its appearance. Only the careful work of grafting in living limbs is allowed, and only the Lord can do it. 'Come here, you who are the Lord's little ones,' Spurgeon pleaded and with the same breath warned, 'but stay far from here you unbelievers and unregenerate!'[14]

For this reason the membership process was approached carefully. It included an interview with an elder, an interview with the pastor, a visitation from appointed church officers, and an investigation of their character subsequent to their professed conversion, a testimony before the church with a corresponding vote of reception, receiving the right hand of fellowship, and then reception of the Lord's Supper. The initial interviews were conducted carefully; over 15,000 summary records were kept of the findings. On this initial

---

14. MTP 20:1167: 'Additions to the Church.'

interview depended the probable success of the remaining steps, but the process could be slowed or entirely halted along the way.

Short glimpses of the life of London permeate these conversion summaries and show the wide variety of backgrounds of those who came to hear Spurgeon and were led to conversion under his ministry. Hannah Wyncoll mentions 'servants, crossing sweepers, hatters, bookbinders, coopers in the docks, tailors, and candle and pottery factory workers.' Also, she noted the wide variety of religious backgrounds of the interviewees, from hardened atheism to formalized state-church members, to tender, consistent, and devoted Sunday School attendees.

Examples of final evaluations in some of these interviews shows the need for spiritual insight in such a stewardship. Most of the reports were from 150 to 200 words. This one was over 1,000 words and began 'This man until eight months ago was an infidel and blasphemer, a tavern lounger, and mocker of religion and religious people; a hater of Baptists more than any other denomination, and of the people of New Park Street more than any other Baptist. No name seems to have been too bad either for them or their pastor.' Then after a substantial narrative of the effects of Spurgeon's preaching, the interviewer summarized: 'Mr Spurgeon's *hard* thrust had evidently been made *home* thrusts by the Holy Spirit. The word was a hammer, blow followed blow. He struggled, writhed, rebelled, still blow followed blow, until he was fairly compelled to give in. Verily there is nothing too hard for the Lord. Let sovereign grace be exalted, world without end.' The interviewer, Thomas Moor, noted, 'I do apologise for making this report so long and will endeavour to avoid a like transgression in the future.' Spurgeon added, 'Not a bit too long! A most blessed case' (22-26).

Another: 'A bookbinder. Was not attending any place of worship but rather opposed to religion. ... No concert room now, no playhouse, the Word of God his chief delight, the people of God his best companions. Wishes to be baptized to shew his love to Christ. I was much pleased with his case and with pleasure gave him a card' (66, 67). Another: 'I questioned this young man very closely upon many of the doctrines and found him for the most part to have now clear views of truth, and I believe him to be sincere. With pleasure, I gave a card' (114).

Another: 'She is very much tried at home with an ungodly father and mother, especially her father who opposes her continually, and has threatened to turn her out of doors if she is baptized. She still, however, wishes to come, and having given me clear evidence of the work of grace in her heart, gave her a card (129). Another: 'She finds prayer a privilege, and the Bible a pleasure to read. She now loves the things and persons she did not once, and hates those she once loved. She wishes to be baptized out of love to Christ and obedience to His command' (129). Another: 'I hardly know what to do with such a case and asked Brother Cook to see her. I quite agree with him that she is a child of God though very much harassed by the enemy, and gave her a card' (138).[15]

At a church meeting in May 1861, several persons were received for baptism and Spurgeon included a note in the 'Meeting Book' accompanying the names. 'There are several very wonderful cases among those above in which sin has abounded, and the grace of God has superabounded. The two marked X were harlots, may they be Rahabs. The brother marked ./. was a very violent infidel, but by the Holy Ghost has received the faith of God's elect. The Lord be praised.'[16]

Baptists have historically sought to guard the principle of regenerate church membership not only at the front door by admitting only the regenerate to baptism, but also by maintaining discipline to exclude those who eventually demonstrate a lifestyle inconsistent with the gospel. Lack of engagement in ministry could result in dismissal. Spurgeon said, 'There are some added

---

15. Hannah Wyncoll, ed. *Wonders of Grace: Original Testimonies of Converts during Spurgeon's Early Years*. The numbers beside the quotes in the text are the page numbers.
16. Ibid., p. 140.

who increase the numbers but not the life; they add only dead weight.' Spurgeon preached about the need for all members of the congregation to be about the business of the church. Some, however, appeared indolent. 'I wonder whether we shall ever have a day such as the bees celebrate in its due season.' Recalling the remarkable scene of nature, Spurgeon described it in application to the unproductive in his congregation. 'You may, perhaps, have seen them dismissing the unproductive bees. It is a remarkable sight. They say to themselves, "Here are a lot of drones, eating our honey, but never making any. Let us turn them out." There is a dreadful buzz, is there not? But out they go.' Spurgeon professed that he personally did not intend to make such a buzz, but others might. 'If ever those who do work for Christ should burn with a holy indignation against do-nothings, some of you will find the place too hot for you! I am sorrowfully afraid that it will thin my congregation and lessen the number of church members.'[17]

Attitudes and words that sir up strife, dissension, and unwarranted dissatisfaction would make a person undesirable for membership. 'When I hear professors railing at the churches to which they belong,' Spurgeon had observed, 'when I see disunion and disaffection among church members, I can well understand that the Lord never added them! And it would be a great mercy to the church if the Lord would take them away.' And take them away He would by the authority He has invested in the elders and congregation for just such occasions.

Doctrinal deviation, persisted in and fomented within the congregation, would result in dismissal. Practically, Spurgeon had virtually no occasion for such discipline at the Met. 'I have sometimes heard a rumour that some one brother has been heretical on a certain point,' Spurgeon reported, 'but it never came in my way so that I knew it to be a fact, or if I did it was after the wanderer had found it best to go elsewhere.' He never considered himself to be like

---

17. MTP 35:2114: 'The Burden of the Word of the Lord.'

a 'terrier dog sniffing for rats to find out everybody who was a little queer in his thinking.' In fact, with scarce half a dozen exceptions, the people 'have remained faithful to the orthodox faith and to the old-fashioned truths of the gospel'.[18]

As a matter of principle, however, Spurgeon knew that sometimes such discipline could be necessary. He saw in the minute books an occasion when John Gill confronted the error of immediate and imputed sanctification that involved a denial of progressive sanctification. In Dr Gill's hand was written that the church had agreed that 'to deny the internal Sanctification of the Spirit, as a principle of Divine Grace and Holiness worked in the heart' until the day of Christ 'is a grievous error' that 'renders persons unfit for church communion'. Any who had embraced the error, therefore, were 'forthwith excluded from it'.

Doctrinal errors of such a dangerous sort were material for church discipline because, in Spurgeon's words, 'this is one of the benefits of church discipline when we are enabled to carry it out under God – that it nips error in the very bud – and thus those who as yet are not infected are kept from it by the blessed Providence of God through the instrumentality of the Church!'

Issues of moral fallenness were dealt with discreetly and with great care and tenderness with the intention of restoration – as in all cases of discipline. In some cases, the elders must do the work apart from the congregation's participation in any detailed way, but only with the general knowledge that an unrepentant person had been removed from membership.

Two Ordinances

'The outward ordinances of the Christian religion are but two, and those two are exceedingly simple,' Spurgeon affirmed, 'yet neither of them has escaped human alteration,' he lamented, adding, 'and, alas! Much mischief has been wrought, and much of precious teaching

---

18. Ernest LeVos, p. 48.

has been sacrificed by these miserable perversions.'[19] In spite of the simple clarity of New Testament baptism, both the mode and the recipient of baptism had been changed. The Lord's Supper likewise had undergone so many alterations, additions, redefinitions, and insertions that its original simplicity and clearly-stated purpose had been smothered. Spurgeon warned, in light of this, 'never either to add to or take from the Word of God so much as a single jot or tittle.' The only safe stance is to keep to the foundation of Scripture which never mentions baptism or the Supper except in the context of conscious and conscientious faith. 'You as sinners have to exercise faith in Christ before you have anything to do with believers' baptism; you have to come to Christ Himself before you are qualified to come to the Lord's table.'[20]

Spurgeon never declined from his strong conviction of believers' baptism by immersion. Utterly rejecting any sacramental efficacy in its administration, Spurgeon pointed to the completed work of Christ as set forth in this emblem, 'the instructive symbol of the new birth, which new birth consists in passing, by death and resurrection, into newness of life.'[21] He preached, 'Baptism sets forth the death, burial, and resurrection of Christ, and our participation therein.' Spurgeon saw it as signifying 'our representative union with Christ' in that His death, burial and resurrection 'was on our behalf.' Baptism 'sets forth a creed' of personal trust in the meritorious nature of His passion. Also, the ordinance speaks to 'our realized union with Christ … as a matter of our experience.' If we are indeed members of His body, we have experienced a 'manner of dying, or being buried, of rising, and of living in Christ.'[22] The ordinance is sent to us from on high and any alteration of it is treason and blasphemy. Believing that baptism is immersion, and that of believers only, Spurgeon would consider himself 'a criminal

---

19. SEE 10:307.
20. SEE 10:326.
21. SEE 10:317.
22. MTP 27:1627: 'Baptism – A Burial.'

in the sight of God if I should give it to any' but believers and in any way other than immersion.

Equally clear must be the administration of the Lord's Supper. Jesus ordained the use of bread and wine. By what authority does the church of Rome withhold the cup from the laity? It is blasphemous so to do. Spurgeon considered that practice 'an act of high treason against the Majesty of Heaven'. Also, the admission of any to the Supper 'who have not made a profession of their faith and of their repentance, and who do not declare themselves to be the true children of God' is a direct contravention of the fellowship realized in the Supper.[23] 'None are invited to come but those who are already saved.'[24]

Spurgeon believed in the symbolic memorial concept of the Lord's Supper with a strong affirmation of Christ's spiritual, not carnal presence. Equally with the emphasis that the bread and wine are emblems and that 'it is a simple memorial festival, that is all,'[25] he stated, 'The spiritual feeding upon the incarnate God, this is what we mean.' Spurgeon spoke of entering into a 'fellowship of the most intense and mysterious kind; not merely eating with Him, but eating Him; not merely receiving from Him, but receiving Him.' While rejecting carnal presence, Spurgeon affirmed the 'real presence of Christ'. This real presence was a spiritual presence 'but that reality is none the less real because it is spiritual; and only spiritual men can discern it.'[26] This 'spiritual presence' is bound up in the purposeful remembrance enjoined by Christ, that in doing this, recipients are instructed by Christ, 'This do in remembrance of me.' This remembrance involves everything about the redemptive work from incarnation to ascension and session. In this mental concentration on the biblical record of Christ and His fully substitutionary work, the Spirit glorifies Christ in our hearts and anew we feast on His

23. NPSP 4:170.
24. SEE 10:305.
25. SEE 10:328.
26. SEE 10:334

redemptive accomplishment. 'Never did any soul truly remember Christ without its faith growing.'[27]

In light of that, Spurgeon saw the Supper as a means of serious examination of spiritual life. In fact, on occasions, when Spurgeon was aware of wrongdoing on the part of a potential communicant, 'I have prevented the wrongdoer from sitting down with us.'[28] Certainly if there is no salvation, then no Supper; but if bitterness, grudges, personal sin unrepented, flippancy, jealousy, or an unloving spirit are prominent, or present, one should not eat and drink a condemnation of conscience and discipline to himself.

> Deacons and elders of the church, you must examine yourselves, because you have known church officers who have brought disgrace upon the offices that they have filled. And you, Sunday school teachers, open-air preachers, tract-distributors, and the like – and you, members of the church – however useful you may be, and however highly you may be respected by your fellow members, I beseech you, nevertheless, shirk not this duty, but let each one examine himself ere he comes to sit down at the table of the Lord.[29]

The most pungent element of the meaning of the Supper for Spurgeon was substitution. All of it points to the atoning work of Jesus on the cross. 'That is the great end and objective of the Lord's Supper, – to set forth – to tell out anew – to proclaim afresh the death of our Lord Jesus Christ.'[30] Our partaking of the elements symbolize His pain, that the death was violent, that we are the beneficiaries of it, and that it was substitutionary.

Spurgeon practiced 'fencing the table' for spiritual reasons: 'There are some of you who must not come to the table of communion because you do not love Christ.'[31] 'If you will not give up sin, if you

---

27. For a sermon on this memorial aspect of the Supper, see 'In Remembrance,' SEE 10:339-50.
28. SEE 10:320.
29. SEE 10:321.
30. SEE 10:298.
31. SEE 10:315.

have even one pet sin that you still determine to keep, you are a traitor to Christ, and you have no more right to come to His table than Judas Iscariot had.'[32] He did not, however, limit participation to his church only, nor even to Baptists only. He had pledged as much to his mother in the letter of June 1850 and maintained this commitment until his death. He seems to have intensified his sense of unity with the whole body of Christ, the full number of the elect spread throughout Christian denominations and across the globe. Giving the Supper in 1890, embedded within Spurgeon's spiritual perception in taking the Supper was a sense of communion 'not only with this church, large as it is, not merely with the members of one denomination (I wish there were no denominations),' but with the entire body of Christians, 'freely inviting all who belong to any part of the visible church.' He embraced the thought that in that very meal on that very night he would have fellowship with 'the brethren in the Congo, with the brethren in India, with the brethren in the United States, of all names, and sorts, and ages, and ranks.'[33]

Two Offices

Baptists accepted two offices in the local church and none outside of it. So did Spurgeon. Without deacons, the church 'would be bereaved of her most valiant sons; their loss would be the shaking of the pillars of our spiritual house, and would cause a desolation on every side.' He blessed God for hard-working deacons who cared for the temporal needs of the church.

The elders were the second office. They cared for the spiritual needs of the church. Spurgeon knew that the work would have been impossible and the church would have existed as a mere sham if it had not been for the scriptural and most expedient office of the eldership. He believed his elders had gained the respect, esteem, and love of the church. He believed other Baptist Churches should

---

32. SEE 10:324.
33. SEE 10:334.

follow their example in this matter, and in doing so would find the effects to be good.[34]

Mission

Seek the Lost. Preaching on Gospel Missions around 1856, Spurgeon announced, 'We feel persuaded that all of you are of one mind in this matter; that it is the absolute duty, as well as the eminent privilege, of the church to proclaim the gospel to the world.'[35] God will not do this work apart from the use of the means that He Himself has ordained and instructed to be used. This involves the Church in a mission until Christ comes or until every single sinner has bowed the knee to King Jesus.

The Metropolitan Tabernacle, therefore, housed the church in that place and became a location from which the gospel labors of the church could be done. The church existed to worship the triune God, but the most prominent evidence of true worship was the involvement in one of the scores of ministries designed to penetrate different segments of the complex London culture with the gospel. Tract distribution, street preaching, benevolent agencies, orphanages, visitation to homes, Sunday School teaching, and the annual butchers' meal – all of these pointed to the necessity of reaching the lost.

Spurgeon also found that the church was the best place for the training of a future ministry. J. C. Carlile, a former student at the College during Spurgeon's days, wrote in 1933: 'The college has always been a missionary institution.' None could attend but those who already had two years of pastoral labors. It began in 1856 with a single student, T. W. Medhurst. Spurgeon, who had heard complaints of his crude manner of preaching in the streets, knew that he must give him education when Medhurst resisted Spurgeon's attempt to curb his zeal by saying, 'I must preach, sir; and I shall preach unless you cut off my head.'[36] Carlile recorded,

---

34. MTP 7:380: 'Meeting of Our Own Church.'
35. SS 1:321.
36. *Autobiography*, 1:388.

'In ten years the college men had baptized 20,676 persons. The gross increase in their churches was 30,677. The students went into districts where no Free Churches existed; many of them began their work by holding open-air services in the market-place or at the street corner.'[37] Spurgeon made no secret of his special affection for the Pastors' College. It had the potential, fully realized, of multiplying his own passion for the church's high calling of preaching the gospel of Jesus Christ to the nations.

Liberty

At the laying of the cornerstone of the Metropolitan Tabernacle in 1859, the deacons presented a brief history of the church and an *apologia* for Baptists. Spurgeon embraced the sentiment with gusto, matched only by his scorn for the idea of an 'established church'. Christ alone has established the Church and it is maintained by Him, succored by Him, sustained by Him, and its members are drawn into its fellowship by Him. A church established by a government presents not only a confusing contradiction but should be disestablished as soon as possible. When popery was cast off, 'full liberty of conscience was neither granted by the legislators, nor understood generally by the people.' Only Baptists grasped and sought, even suffered for the 'great principle of unrestricted religious liberty'. They alone 'scrupulously maintained it, and pioneered the way for its popular apprehension.' They were accounted schismatics, had to meet together by stealth, and went from house to house seeking a safe place for worship. Spurgeon contended that 'No novelty whatever led to the distinctness of our communion. No factious spirit induces us to perpetuate it. As a protest against an innovation still fostered in Christian churches, we preserve the inscription of "Baptist" on our banners.' Though holding in common a large body of doctrine with other faithful believers in other denominations, 'we desire now,' Spurgeon continued, 'as ever,

---

37. Carlile, pp. 172, 174.

in our own fellowship, to maintain the pureness of that polity which is formed upon the model of the church at Jerusalem.'[38]

Another Denomination?

Spurgeon's influence on and activity within Baptist life in London and across England and beyond was remarkable. In March of 1866, the 'Notices' section of *The Sword and the Trowel* carried reports that are typical of Spurgeon's involvement in the ministry for the growth of the Baptist cause. A student at the Pastors' College, Mr R. Swann, had been involved in open air preaching in 'a much neglected district' and a congregation had been raised. In February 1866, a 'spacious and elegant chapel, named Peniel Tabernacle,' was opened near Camden Town. The proceedings to open the tabernacle were well attended and involved the participation of leaders in Baptist life as well as evangelicals from other connections. Spurgeon made an appeal for 'help from those who are charitably disposed towards such efforts for the extension of the kingdom of their Lord'.

In the same report, Spurgeon mentioned the 'meetings of the Association at Bloomsbury Chapel' as being 'very happy and useful'. This meeting, largely at the instigation of Spurgeon, was the re-founding of the London Baptist Association. Upon Spurgeon's nomination, Mr W. Brock was elected president, whose nomination had been seconded by Baptist Noel and supported by W. Landels.

Brock was a highly successful and celebrated pastor of Bloomsbury Chapel, something of a Spurgeon before Spurgeon, a prodigy as a young preacher and highly successful as an energetic and resourceful pastor. He remained a leading voice among the Baptists until his death in 1875. Noel's entrance into Baptist life had been quite controversial and highly publicized as he converted from Anglicanism to Baptist convictions and left prestigious appointments and a promising future in the established church. When Landels a decade later was elected President of the Baptist Union, Spurgeon

---

38. NPSP 5:268.

anointed him as Mr Greatheart, 'brave as a lion and true as steel,' for his courageous address affirming the distinctives of Baptist doctrine. Spurgeon looked upon the indulgence granted Baptists by the Congregationalists as 'tinctured with contempt'. Following the transparent honesty of Landels, Spurgeon said that Baptists possess 'a deposit of sacred truth to defend, and we shall not hesitate to battle for it.'[39] Spurgeon noted: 'Intimations were thrown out, and some promises made, in reference to the erection of a new Chapel, which is much needed in order that the Baptist denomination may be fairly represented in Bedford.'

As Spurgeon increased in popularity and trained very effective ministers who were used of God to revive destitute churches and plant scores of new ones, an American observer, Coit Tyler, writing for the *New York Independent*, opined that the Baptist sect of 'Spurgeonism' was 'covering all the land with its *network* of moral power'. Spurgeonite preachers, who loved and imitated Spurgeon, were everywhere.[40] Soon, the article suggested, alongside 'Wesleyanism' another sect entitled 'Spurgeonism' would emerge, a separate sect from the Baptists.

The writer had no idea how reprehensible that entire idea of a Spurgeonite sect was to the London pastor. Though every Baptist church was independent, 'to charge us with separating from the general organisation of the religious world, and even of the Baptist denomination, is to perpetrate an unfounded libel.' He wanted no new gospel, no new object, no novel spirit. He loved Christ better than any so-called sect, truth above any party, but was in 'open union with the Baptists for the very reasons that we cannot endure isolation'.

Just a few months later, another article on 'Spurgeonism' appeared, this time accusing Spurgeon of taking too active a role, even a purposely dominant one, within the Baptist Union. With obvious frustration, Spurgeon gave this assurance: 'It was never our wish to

---

39. S&T, 1876, p. 285.
40. S&T, 1866, p. 138.

appear to be alienated from our esteemed Baptist brethren, for whom in proportion to our personal knowledge of them our affectionate esteem increases; but far less have we it in our mind to compose any grasping of the whole system of the denomination, or to obtain or exercise any predomination of influence in it.' He noted that his increased participation among his Baptist brethren had met only with a hearty fellowship. He had no intention to dominate or to create tension, much less separation. 'So long as we can all of us live for Christ, and as a community maintain the purity of the gospel of Jesus, and a hallowed practical zeal for the Master's glory, it can little matter to any man among us whose influence may be most helpful to promote our prosperity.' Spurgeon expressed his conviction that 'never were our Baptist brethren more vigorous in spiritual life; and that our present unity and zeal is no more due to any one man than this delightful springtime is due to the birds whose songs proclaim it.'

A Painful Parting – But still a Baptist

At the Downgrade, some Baptists in America thought that he had withdrawn from being a Baptist. He wrote some friends to assure them that this certainly was not the case, and papers published his description of the theological difficulties of the Baptist Union and reasons for calling it the Downgrade. After seeing this, *The Central Baptist* wrote: 'The famous London preacher is, if possible, more of a Baptist now than ever, and his alleged "withdrawal" was due to his firm and unflinching adherence to Baptist tenets.' They closed the article by saying: 'These are the facts as fully as we have been able to obtain them, and in the light of these statements, every Baptist and every lover of truth, of whatever name, must commend the action of Mr Spurgeon.'[41]

---

41. *The Central Baptist*, 3 November 1887, p. 4.

4

'THEY DO NOT PLAY AT PREACHING'

. . . .

In April 1850, Spurgeon wrote his mother about the man that she heard preach regularly: 'I often think of you poor starving creatures, falling for the bony rhetoric and oratory which he gives you. What a mercy that you are not dependent upon him for spiritual comfort! I hope you will soon give up following that empty cloud without rain, that type-and-shadow preacher, for I don't think there is much substance.'[1] The very next month, Spurgeon indicated to his mother his own growing sense of finding usefulness through preaching: 'I hope you may one day have cause to rejoice, should you see me, the unworthy instrument of God, preaching to others.'[2]

Though Spurgeon loved books, he loved the preached Word more. Reflecting on his own conversion, Spurgeon remarked: 'The revealed Word awakened me, but it was the preached Word that saved me; and I must ever attach peculiar value to the hearing of the truth, for by it I received the joy and peace in which my soul delights.'[3] In 1875, Spurgeon reminisced about his early fascination with the pulpit and its potential for transformative power and confessed, 'Before I had ever entered a pulpit, the thought had

---

1. To his mother, 20 April 1850.
2. *Autobiography*, 1:118.
3. Ibid., 1:86.

occurred to me that I should one day preach sermons which would be printed.' As one of the most celebrated and effective pulpiteers in Christian history, Spurgeon's early contemplations about preaching bore remarkable fruit. It was not merely a phenomenon of nature, but the result of careful thinking and purposeful reflection on the call to preach.

Gifts and Calling Requisite

Spurgeon looked on the ministry as 'a high and honourable calling when a man is really fitted for it; but without the necessary qualifications it must be little better than sheer slavery.'[4] Contemplating the seriousness of gospel ministry and the lightness with which some ministers receive their task, Spurgeon warned: 'He that does not find his ministry a burden now will find it a burden hereafter, which will sink him lower that the lowest hell. A ministry that never burdens the heart and the conscience in this life, will be like a millstone about a man's neck in the world to come.'[5] Not only would an individual chafe presently, and perhaps eternally, under the burden of a ministry to which he was not called, but the church itself would be endangered. 'When I think upon the all but infinite mischief which may result from a mistake as to our vocation for the Christian pastorate,' Spurgeon warned, 'I feel overwhelmed with fear lest any of us should be slack in examining our credentials.' Though one genuinely called should seize the task with gusto and determination, Spurgeon would 'rather that we stood too much in doubt, and examined too frequently, than that we should become cumberers of the ground. There are not lacking many exact methods by which a man may test his call to the ministry if he earnestly desires to do so.'[6]

He warned that some might be fascinated with the public nature of the preacher's office and therefore cautioned 'all young men not

---

4. S&T, March 1883, p. 109.
5. SEE 12:263.
6. *Lectures*, 1:23.

to mistake whim for inspiration, and a childish preference for a call of the Holy Spirit.'[7] It is no violation of the priesthood of all believers that God set aside some to be 'successors of those who, in olden times, were moved of God to declare His Word, to testify against transgression, and to plead His cause.' Unless the Spirit of the prophets rests on a preacher, 'the mantle which we wear is nothing but a rough garment to deceive.' A person should never take up the ministry 'without having a solemn conviction that the Spirit from on high has set you apart; for, if you do, the blood of souls will be found in your skirts.'[8]

Within the call of the Holy Spirit are embedded certain gifts, convictions, and traits of character. These certainly will grow in clarity and profundity but are present in seed form as a constituent element of a true call to preach the gospel.

A Saving Experience of Grace

The first necessary trait, therefore, of a call to ministry is a saving experience of the grace of God. 'Whatever his natural gifts, whatever his mental powers may be, he is utterly out of court for spiritual work if he has no spiritual life.' He is like a blind professor of optics, a dumb master of elocution, or a deaf critic of symphonic music. He painted a graphic picture of those who took upon the role of preacher without saving grace. 'It will be well for some if they shall be able to wash their hands of the blood of souls,' Spurgeon warned, 'for verily in the cells of eternal condemnation there are heard no yells of horror more appalling than the shrieks of damned ministers.'[9]

For Spurgeon, a saving experience of the gospel included both cognitive and spiritual knowledge of the doctrines of grace. For effective, God-glorifying ministry, one who proclaims the gospel must see the connections of grace permeating and giving unity

---

7. *Autobiography*, 1:19.
8. SEE 5:465.
9. *The Saint and His Saviour*, pp. 143-44.

to each aspect of God's saving work. Spurgeon believed that the experience of grace, properly understood, would fortify a man's ministry to preach without compromise. In considering how one should approach the doctrines of grace in preaching, he asked, 'Why should this particular truth be concealed? Are we ashamed of it?' If that were the case, then 'let us revise our creed; but in the name of common honesty let us hide nothing which we believe.' All of revelation sheds light on what is to be believed and, therefore, what is to be proclaimed. 'The more light the better. The more fully truth is made known the more surely will good come of it.' Though some may think it the better part of wisdom to hide such strong, potentially offensive doctrines, Spurgeon affirmed that the doctrines of grace commanded 'the enthusiasm of my whole being'.[10]

Beyond that, a preacher must feel the power of it. In Spurgeon's view, superior esteem for the worthiness and power of the gospel must arise from the engagement of the soul with the propositions of Scripture. Primarily, the Bible is about Christ as the only fit person to be Savior. The first measure of the worthiness of the gospel, therefore, is the superior, yea infinite, worth of the one person in whom it most essentially consists – Jesus of Nazareth, the Christ. There is no more exalted concept in all thought than all that is included in the biblical presentation of the God-man who laid down His life for rebellious creatures.

In 1859, Spurgeon laid out the irreducible necessity of our seeing all gifts of grace culminating in Christ:

> Election is a good thing, ... but we are elect in Christ Jesus. Adoption is a good thing; ... ay, but we are adopted in Christ Jesus and made joint-heirs with Him. Pardon is a good thing – ... ay, but we are pardoned through the precious blood of Jesus. Justification – is not that a noble thing, to be robed about with a perfect righteousness? – ay, but we are justified in Jesus. To be preserved – is not that a precious thing? – ay;

---

10. SEE 7:35.

but we are preserved in Christ Jesus, and kept by His power even to the end. Perfection – who shall say that this is not precious? But He hath raised us up and made us sit together with Him in heavenly places in Jesus Christ – so that Christ must be good positively, for He is all the best things in one.[11]

Second, and correlative to the first, the Bible presents the final purpose of the gospel, not as terminating on anything temporal or finite, but on glorifying God. In the gospel we see an impressive and connected display of His attributes impossible to attain otherwise. Taking his cue from the Westminster Shorter Catechism, Spurgeon spoke during his last year of ministry on 'Man's chief end is to glorify and enjoy God'. He pointed to God's own object in all things, His 'greatest and highest object', is 'to make Himself a glorious and an everlasting name'. Spurgeon felt no urge to apologize for such a self-focus of God in all that He does – creation, providence, revelation, redemption, judgment – for He alone is worthy of such focus, and in that He includes the wellbeing of His creatures. 'It is by the making of that name that men are blessed in the very highest degree, and helped to holiness and happiness.'[12]

A third excellence of the gospel consists of its holy effect in the conversion, forgiveness and transformation of rebels. One must sense in one's own soul the power of Peter's admonition: 'As he who called you is holy, you also be holy in all your conduct, … And if you call on the Father, … conduct yourselves throughout the time of your stay here in fear.' Particularly, the minister himself must feel the sanctifying influence of gospel truth. The prominence of the office might draw many pretenders. Spurgeon saw it himself in those who sought to endear themselves to him, even early in his ministry, in the hopes of getting a recommendation for a position. Such self-serving must be avoided in the ministry, for it is a way of corruption and destruction. 'The world is full of counterfeits, and

---

11. NPSP 5:141.
12. SEE 7:412: 'God's Glorious and Everlasting Name.'

swarms with panderers to carnal self-conceit, who gather around a minister as vultures around a carcass.'[13]

Nothing Else Satisfies

Another abiding aspect of a call to ministry is an inability to give oneself fully to anything other than gospel ministry. Spurgeon recognized that many aspects of gospel ministry were trying to the soul and had all the elements of a death wish. That one thing, however, that put all else in positive context was the moment of preaching. He complained, 'Although I must complain when people expect impossibilities of me,' yet he still found 'the highest enjoyment of my life to be busily engaged for Christ' in preaching. Even though he reported with candor in 1855: 'We have known what it is to totter on the pulpit steps, under a sense that the chief of sinners should scarcely be allowed to preach to others,'[14] he still acknowledged, 'Tell me the day when I do not preach – I will tell you the day in which I am not happy! And the day in which it is my privilege to preach the Gospel and labour for God is generally the day of my peaceful and quiet enjoyment after all.'[15]

Built for the Battle

In his Pastors' College, Spurgeon gave Friday lectures on exposition, illustrations, use of anecdotes, gestures, and vocal production. Not only was preaching a calling, dependent on the Spirit of God for success, but it was an art, a physical endowment, and a stewardship of a gift to be developed. It could and should be improved with knowledge and practice in every aspect of public discourse.

Spurgeon famously pointed out certain physical and vocal characteristics that should be present if one would successfully prosecute a long-term pulpit ministry. Spurgeon in his lectures gave special

---

13. *Lectures* 1:4.
14. SS 1:12.
15. MTP 45:2607: 'Foretastes of the Heavenly Life' (Sermon preached initially in 1857).

attention to elements of delivery. A man could have excellent content, but if jumbled and mangled by a bumbling delivery, the message would be shrouded.

In the use of the voice, any peculiarities that make one difficult to understand should be corrected. Poor teeth make for poor articulation, so take care of your teeth. Pay attention to patterns of speech and make sure you don't drop the energy of speaking at the end of a sentence, causing the loss of the last words. Don't use rhythms that become predictable and thus distracting. Avoid what he called 'servant girlified dawdling in speech'. Bawling and roaring will do no good. The people will not listen, and you will wear yourself out. Spurgeon claimed that he could whisper in the Tabernacle so as to be heard and understood in every place. The following testimony to his voice verifies the claim:

> His voice was wonderful. It swept in distinct, flexible, sweet strong tones, molded into faultless articulation through the great tabernacle, reaching easily and apparently without the slightest effort six thousand hearers, and riveting their entire attention from the first sentence. There was an indefinable quality in his voice, as is the case with all great orators, that made it captivating and thrilling. Perhaps it was his tremendous and irresistible personality that spoke through it. Whatever it was it would conquer a vast multitude in an instant. This made him a peerless speaker.[16]

Accordingly, idiosyncrasies of speech should be corrected whenever possible. He recognized the variety of dialects that existed in the counties around London and pointed out the peculiarly distracting aspect of each, having something of their 'rustic diet in their mouths'. By this he referred to the 'calves of Essex, the swine of Berkshire, or the runts of Suffolk,' and added his opinion that the unmistakable dialects of Yorkshire or Somerset were equally amusing. For one who defended naturalness and disliked affectation, Spurgeon was as relentless as he was merciless

---

16. Northrop, p. 607, citing a tribute from 'The Christian at Work'.

in hunting down unpleasant sounds that would dominate any message that came through the lips.

Sometimes comprehensible delivery depended on correcting the local color of one's vocal patterns. In some counties, men's throats seem to be 'furred up, like long-used teakettles.' Others have a sharp resonance that pangs like brass music 'with a vicious metallic sound'. Although these sounds may be amusing in their context, Spurgeon had never enjoyed them in the pulpit. 'A sharp discordant squeak, like a rusty pair of scissors, is to be got rid of at all hazards; so also is a thick, inarticulate utterance in which no word is complete, but nouns, adjectives, and verbs are made into a kind of hash.' Humorously, Spurgeon would mimic each of these in his lectures including a kind of 'ghostly speech in which a man talks without using his lips, ventriloquising most horribly.'[17]

While the teeth were important for articulation, equally important were characteristics of robust vocal production connected with chest and lungs. In the days before electronic amplification, vocal endurance and projection were necessary as a part of the minister's apparatus. Spurgeon, therefore, looked for men not only with a sincere and tender heart, but with large chests and vocal cords that could produce pleasantly and perseveringly.

These physical traits, however, would be useless apart from the passion and conviction of the renewed nature. The minister himself is his own best tool and he must, therefore, cultivate his bodily gifts as a fit vehicle for his spiritual life and calling. 'If I want to preach the gospel, I can only use my own voice; therefore, I must train my vocal powers,' he told his students at the Pastors' College. 'I can only think with my own brains, and feel with my own heart, and therefore I must educate my intellectual and emotional faculties.' These will be expanded to their fullest usefulness in tandem with spiritual growth, for 'I can only weep and agonise for souls in my

---

17. *Lectures* 1:121.

own renewed nature, therefore must I watchfully maintain the tenderness which was in Christ Jesus.'[18]

Preach With Interest

Combining his uncanny knowledge of human nature with a deep appreciation of how Jesus and the prophets profitably used anecdotes and illustrations, Spurgeon advocated their use in preaching. He referred to a wealthy tailor whose success was credited to his always having put a knot in his thread. So is an illustration – a knot in the thread to keep it from slipping away. The greatest natural ability must be combined with devoted industry, not only for the proper exposition of a text, but for arresting the attention of drowsy, energiless, distracted listeners. He listed seven uses of these helps in preaching.

First, they 'interest the mind and secure the attention of our hearers'. Second, such material 'renders our preaching life-like and vivid'. Jesus used the presence of children, the fragile beauty of a lily, and the free-flying raven, to give vivid points to His message and forever seal to the mind of His listener a spiritual point from a daily experience of the listener. Third, dull understanding will grasp both doctrine and duty more readily through an excellent illustration or anecdote. Fourth, the reasoning of induction is engaged in the use of illustrations particularly when they employ the quick accumulation of facts, for instance, of many examples of answered prayer. Fifth, these literary devices 'help the memory to grasp the truth'. Sixth, 'illustrations and anecdotes are useful because they frequently arouse the feelings.' Sometimes deeply moved feelings can make a point that 'closely reasoned arguments' or the 'most eloquent harangue' could never approach. The seventh justification given by Spurgeon was that 'they catch the ear of the utterly careless'. The preacher, in light of these helpful usages of illustrations, must rouse his faculties and put forth all his energy to 'get the people to heed that which they are

---

18. *Lectures* 1:2. 'The Minister's Self-Watch.'

so slow to regard'. He must read much, and study hard. To make a thoroughly efficient preacher, a man who has 'the best natural ability' must supplement it 'with the greatest imaginable industry'. Only in this way can one 'do much service for God among this crooked and perverse generation'.[19]

Preach the Word

Illustrations always should serve the apt exposition of the Word of God. All preaching must develop a clear proposition from the sole authority of Scripture. The sermon may give an extended discussion of a topic or a doctrine, but all the points must be founded biblically. We have no other recourse in preaching, for the knowledge of salvation in Christ is a matter of pure revelation.

Spurgeon, near the end of his ministry, reaffirmed his conviction: 'We are further resolved that we will preach nothing but the Word of God.' He asserted, as he looked at the spiritual devastation wrought by higher criticism: 'The alienation of the masses from hearing the gospel is largely to be accounted for by the sad fact that it is not always the gospel that they hear if they go to places of worship; and all else falls short of what their souls need.'[20] Man's wisdom or philosophy has done nothing either to produce it or understand it. Only the Word of God leads to the knowledge of God and eternal life. 'A babe in grace taught by the Spirit of God may know the mind of the Lord concerning salvation, and find its way to heaven by the guidance of the Word alone. But be it profound or simple, that is not the question; it is the Word of God, and is pure, unerring truth. Here is infallibility, and nowhere else.' So why would a preacher preach anything else?[21]

Spurgeon knew of nothing else to preach. Whether on the offense or the defense, our strategy and content must be found in 'the volume of inspiration'. Should others have another source,

19. *Lectures* 3:31-53.
20. *The Greatest Fight in the World*, p. 64.
21. MTP 20:1208: 'Infallibility – Where To Find It and How To Use It.'

Spurgeon confessed, 'I have none.' I have nothing else to preach when I have got through with this book,' he affirmed, and continued, 'Indeed, I can have no wish to preach at all if I may not continue to expound the subjects which I find in these pages. What else is worth preaching?' God's truth is the only treasure to seek, and 'the Scripture is the only field in which we dig for it'.

His own understanding of the various sermonic styles and their relation to exposition he summarized in the preface to *Commenting and Commentaries*. Spurgeon placed himself as third person in the position of a 'judicious critic' of contemporary preaching. Such a critic probably would 'complain that many sermons are deficient in solid instruction, Biblical exposition, and Scriptural argument.' Rather than fleshy, they are flashy; rather than solid, they are clever; and rather than impressive, they are entertaining. Doctrine is barely discernible, and the brilliant harangues embody no soul-food. This critic, if as forthright and honest as Spurgeon himself, would 'propose that homilies should flow out of texts, and should consist of a clear explanation, and an earnest enforcement of the truths which the texts distinctly teach.' He would advocate expository preaching as the great need of the day and as most apt to protect against rising error while providing spiritual edification. The critic would not 'unite in any indiscriminate censuring of hortatory addresses, or topical sermons,' nor would he agree with the 'demand that every discourse should be limited to the range of its text, nor even that it should have a text at all.' Nevertheless, he would continue to subscribe to the proposition, 'that more expository preaching is greatly needed, and that all preachers would be the better if they were more able expounders of the inspired Word.'[22]

Some would be surprised at Spurgeon's advocacy of expository preaching. Though many of his sermons deal with doctrinal subjects, or use a verse as a theme, one must not underestimate Spurgeon's commitment to continuous exposition. 'What are sermons but

---

22. *Commenting and Commentaries,* p. iii.

commentaries?' Spurgeon asked; 'At least they ought to be.' He advocated that the minister should employ the best commentaries (Puritan!) along with his original study. The goal is a thorough understanding of the Bible through mastering it one book at a time. 'The close, critical, exhaustive investigation of one part best qualifies for a similar examination of another.'[23]

The text must govern the sermon. In 'The Minister's Farewell', preached at Surrey Gardens near the end of his time there, Spurgeon summarized the preacher's task in terms of declaring 'the whole counsel of God – to gather up ten thousand things into one – I think it is needful that when a minister gets his text, he should say what that text means honestly and uprightly.' Many preachers not only avoid dealing with a text but 'get a text and kill it. They wring its neck, then stuff it with some empty notions and present it upon the table for an unthinking people to feed upon.' A preacher does not preach the 'whole counsel of God who does not let God's Word speak for itself in its own pure, simple language.'

Spurgeon could say this with conviction and honesty because a portion of each worship service contained several minutes of unvarnished exposition. Spurgeon insisted, 'Earnestly do I advocate commenting.' The extra study will provide expanding and long-term benefits. 'As a rule,' Spurgeon claimed, 'I spend much more time over the exposition than over the discourse.'[24] He made short pithy comments, not on every verse, but on several, sometimes of a devotional nature, sometimes a brief theological point, sometimes a reminder of the context, sometimes a very practical point from a theologically-loaded text.

Each sermon was usually a doctrinal expansion of one of the verses that had been read in the time of exposition. Following an exposition of John 16:1-33, he preached on John 16:14, 'The Spirit's Office Towards Disciples.' The point was to preach an expansive doctrinal message on how the Spirit glorifies Christ in the lives of

---

23. S&T 1866:94.
24. *Commenting and Commentaries*, p. 24.

disciples. Some of the points in which he had pursued doctrinal and experimental discussion were: 'He gives us more and more debasing views of our own selves'; He honours the person of Christ'; 'The Spirit glorifies Christ in His work'; 'The Holy Spirit exalts Christ in all His offices [of prophet, priest, and king]'; 'Christ is also exalted by the Holy Spirit in His Word.' Under this point, Spurgeon emphasized: 'There are some who think and say that they can do without the Bible; but such think and speak not by the Spirit of God certainly. This is always an infallible test of the work of the Spirit, that he honours God's own Word.' Another point emphasizing the Christocentric purpose of the Spirit's work: 'There is nothing which concerneth Christ which the Spirit of God doth not magnify.' Spurgeon preached four other points on this subject, but they all were an expansion of the ideas set forth in the more formal exposition of the larger passage.

Sermons, therefore, even if without a particular text, must arise from a personal practice of daily exposition and meditation on Scripture, and be firmly grounded in the truth of biblical revelation. He admonished his congregation accordingly. Preaching on 'Unconditional Election' in the first year of his New Park Street ministry, Spurgeon insisted: 'And if you do not see it to be here in the Bible – whatever I may say, or whatever authorities I may plead – I beseech you, as you love your souls, reject it! And if from this pulpit you ever hear things contrary to this sacred Word, remember that the Bible must be first.'

The same fixation on Scripture must dominate the preacher's relation to the sermon. 'God's minister must lie underneath it! We must not stand on the Bible to preach – we must preach with the Bible above our heads.' This is because the Bible lifts us to truths undiscernible by any human gifts of logic or methods of research. It is revealed from heaven and defies our attempts at exhaustive knowledge. Even after preaching with all earnestness and thoroughness, we see that 'the mountain of truth is higher than our eyes can discern – clouds and darkness are round about its summit and we cannot discern its topmost pinnacle. Yet we will try to preach it as well as we can.'[25]

In a sermon on 'Gospel Missions', preached in April 1856, and based on Acts 13:40, Spurgeon admitted candidly: 'I shall not confine myself to the text.' Normally texts are taken for sermons, but Spurgeon intended to preach at large on the subject of 'Gospel Missions'. Spurgeon then preached using a survey of the New Testament on the characteristics of apostolic preaching – mission fervor, earnestness, suffering, zeal – that were present in every age of revival and success of gospel extension in the world. He lamented its apparent absence in his age. He looked for 'men with apostolic zeal', eyes 'like the eyes of the Saviour which could weep over Jerusalem', and those who like Paul could preach with confidence that their faith was settled on absolute realities.[26]

He appealed that one should preach the gospel as set forth in the doctrines of grace, with full confidence that by it souls will be saved. 'How many there are who preach a Gospel which they are afraid will not save souls and therefore they add little bits of their own to it in order, as they think, to win men to Christ?' he asked. He knew preachers 'who preached Calvinism in the morning and Arminianism in the evening because they were afraid God's Gospel would not convert sinners!' Spurgeon clearly revolted against such a practice, contending that the one 'who does not believe God's Gospel is able to save men's souls, does not believe it at all! If God's Truth will not save men's souls, man's lies cannot! If God's Truth will not turn men to repentance, I am sure there is nothing in this world that can!'[27]

Success in preaching is immediately related to unintimidated confidence in the power of the truths of the Word of God. 'When we believe the Gospel to be powerful, then we shall see it is powerful!' To the charge that the display of this confidence made him an egotist and dogmatic, Spurgeon responded: 'Yes, and the young man means to

---

25. NPSP 1:41, 42: 'Unconditional Election.'
26. SS 1:321-23.
27. SS 1:326.

be! He glories in it, he keeps it to himself as one of his peculiar titles, for he does most firmly believe what he preaches!' No faltering words or doubted suppositions should come from the preacher's mouth, but words of full assurance. 'He who has courage enough to grasp the standard and hold it up will be sure enough to find followers!' Like Jesus, he must not speak as the Scribes and Pharisees, but with authority. On the mission field, the business is not to wrangle with the philosophies and religious ideas of the people but to proclaim with authority what 'God has most certainly revealed'. It needs no other foundation than that God has said it. Human logic and reason cannot rise above it. 'We are not to seek to be clever in order to meet them. Leave the men of the world to combat their metaphysical errors. We have merely to say, "This is Truth – he that believes it shall be saved and he that denies it shall be damned." We have no right to come down from the high ground of Divine authoritative testimony.'[28]

The one who preaches with unbelief in his heart will preach unsuccessfully. Timidity, fear and driveling doubt will disarm the preacher of his sword. 'We need to be quite sure of what we preach,' Spurgeon proclaimed. Careless of man's esteem, but with full confidence in God's revealed truth, the gospel proclaimer must take his stand and find that 'God rewards faith and crowns it with His own crown!'[29]

From these first years to the last of his ministry, Spurgeon proclaimed confidence in the Scriptures as essential for effective preaching. Preaching in the Pastors' College in 1880, Spurgeon would brook no uncertainty in preaching the doctrines of Scripture. 'Believing, therefore, that there is such a thing as truth,' he began his major premise, and, he continued, 'such a thing as falsehood,' and observing with infinite urgency that 'there are truths in the Bible, and that the gospel consists in something definite which is to be believed by men,' he concluded 'it becomes us to be decided as to what we teach, and to teach it in a decided manner.'[30]

---

28. SS 1:327f.
29. SS 1:326-28.
30. *Lectures* 2:40.

In 1891, preaching to the men at the Pastors' College Evangelical Association, four years into the Downgrade, Spurgeon asked the attendants, 'Do you think, dear Friend, that you can be wiser than the Holy Spirit? And if His choice must be a wise one, will yours be a wise one if you begin to take of the things of something or somebody else?' Spurgeon was preaching specifically of the biblical revelation of the person and work of Christ. The Spirit's work of revelation and inspiration in the production of Scripture was to take the things of Christ and show them to the apostles, and through them to us. 'You will have the Holy Spirit near you when you are receiving of the things of Christ,' Spurgeon reminded his former students, 'but, as the Holy Spirit is said never to receive anything else, when you are handling other things on the Sabbath, you will be handling them alone.' If that is the case, they will find that 'the pulpit is a dreary solitude, even in the midst of a crowd – if the Holy Spirit is not with you there.'

In that age of increasing infidelity toward the Scripture, Spurgeon set before them two options: 'You may, if you please, think through a theology out of your own vast brain, but the Holy Spirit is not with you there. And, mark you, there are some of us that are resolved to tarry with the things of Christ and keep on dealing with them as far as He enables us to do so!' He envied no one that 'wider range of thought'.

Preach Christ

If a preacher preaches Scripture, then he certainly will preach Christ. From his earliest days, Spurgeon yearned for the preaching of Christ. His first sermon was based on the text in 1 Peter 2:7, 'To you who believe He is precious' (NKJV). During his Waterbeach years, among his early sermons were: 'Christ About His Father's Business,' based on Luke 2:49; 'Christ is All,' based on Colossians 3:11; 'The Lamb and the Lion Conjoined,' based on Revelation 5:5-6; 'The Son's Love to us Compared to God's Love to Him,' based on John 15:9; 'King of Righteousness and Peace,' based on Hebrews 7:2; 'Jesus, the Shower from Heaven,' based on Psalm 72:6; 'The Eloquence of Jesus,' based on John 17:6; 'He Took Not Up Angels,' based on Hebrews 2:16; 'Gethsemane's Sorrow,' based on Matthew 26:38; 'What Think Ye of Christ,' based on Matthew 22:42.

His love for and endless fascination with the themes connected to the person and work of Christ were infused in virtually every sermon. Preaching on 1 Timothy 3:16, Spurgeon summarized: 'Out of these six articles of Paul's creed, they all speak of Christ; from which I gather that if we are to preach the gospel faithfully, we must preach much concerning Jesus Christ. My dear brothers, this must be the first, the middle, and end of our ministry.'[31] He contended that true exposition had not been consummated if it did not find its final resting place in the cross of Christ. In 1856, in 'Christ Crucified', Spurgeon said of the cross of Christ:

> Our meditation upon it enlarges the mind; and as it opens to our soul in successive flashes of glory, we stand astonished at the profound wisdom manifest in it. Ah, dear friends! If ye seek wisdom, ye shall see it displayed in all its greatness; not in the balancing of the clouds, not the firmness of earth's foundations; not in the measured march of the armies of the sky, not in the perpetual motions of the waves of the sea; not in vegetation with all its fairy forms of beauty, not in the animal with its marvelous tissue of nerve, and vein, and sinew; not even in man, that last and loftiest work of the Creator. But turn aside and see this great sight! – an incarnate God upon the cross; a substitute atoning for mortal guilt; a sacrifice satisfying the vengeance of Heaven, and delivering the rebellious sinner. Here is essential wisdom; enthroned, crowned, glorified. Admire, ye men of earth, if ye be not blind; and ye who glory in your learning bend your heads in reverence, and own that all your skill could not have devised a gospel at once so just to God, so safe to man.[32]

In 1874, he still insisted on the same theme as the power of true preaching. In calling for 'a Holy Spirit ministry', Spurgeon

31. SEE 3:17.
32. SS 1:108: 'Christ Crucified.'

lamented that 'many churches would not be content with a ministry whose power would lie solely in the Holy Spirit'. They judge a minister by 'his elaboration of style or beauty of imagery, or degree of culture.' But Spurgeon insisted that true preaching came only in the power of the Spirit; and the power of the Spirit was related immediately to the preaching of Jesus Christ and Him crucified. While many celebrate great oratory, full of human power, but bereft of spiritual conviction, 'Plainness of speech is the perfection of gospel utterance.' A Holy Spirit ministry is 'one which tells men that Jesus is the Christ, and that they have crucified Him – and calls upon them to repent and turn unto the Lord!' Such a minister 'chooses Jesus for His main theme, as Peter did.' Avoiding all attempts at human contrivance and clever manipulation of Scripture, 'Peter went right on setting forth Christ crucified and Christ risen from the dead!' On that basis, the preacher appealed for repentance and public identification with Christ through baptism. 'The man was full of God, and God shone through the man and worked with him! Remission of sins was sought for and was found through repentance and faith in the Lord Jesus Christ by a vast number of souls! May God send to all His Churches a Holy Spirit ministry!'[33]

Because all biblical doctrine eventually led Spurgeon back to Christ and His atoning work, he did not hesitate to engage in a straightforward proclamation of the whole spectrum of systematic theology as a means of preaching the whole Bible as the whole counsel of God. His method of argument, however, for doctrine was not to lay bare the internal rational coherence of the system of doctrine, showing how each part of it implies and necessitates another part. That was the job of Jonathan Edwards, whom Spurgeon studied with great admiration. Spurgeon, however, looked more to the authoritative declamation of doctrine built on the assumption of its carrying its own authority because it is the Word of God.

---

33. MTP 20:1167: 'Additions to the Church.'

'What can our driveling arguments add to the pronouncement of God upon any subject?' he asked. The reinforcement of these announced truths is not to be done by delineating carefully the fusion of ideas within the entire framework of biblical doctrine, but with an assault on the conscience through heart language and a prevailing rhetoric, the abundance of which disarms the objector of any arguments. In a sermon entitled 'Faith', Spurgeon noted: 'Now, there are some gentlemen present who are saying, "Now we shall see whether Mr Spurgeon has any logic in him." No, you won't sirs,' Spurgeon hypothesized his response, 'because I never pretend to exercise it.' He was not arguing for irrationality, but for a more direct channel to affect the heart of his hearer. 'I hope I have the logic which can appeal to men's hearts,' he continued, 'but I am not very prone to use the less powerful logic of the head, when I can win the heart in another manner.' He understood the finer points of logic at least as well as those who 'undertake to censure me'. He believed they should learn how to hold their tongues, 'which is at least a fine part of rhetoric.'

The appeal to the heart that Spurgeon emphasized in his logic spawned the character of his rhetoric. He ignored neither *logos* nor *ethos* in his public discourse, but his major emphasis, and perhaps talent, was *pathos*. 'My argument,' he testified, 'shall be such as, I trust, will appeal to the heart and conscience, although it may not exactly please those who are always so fond of syllogistic demonstration, – who could a hair divide between the west and northwest side.'[34]

In Summary

Preachers of the Word find the calling both a joy and a burden. Contrasting the preachers of orthodoxy with the modernist pulpiteers of the day, Spurgeon could not see that the latter ever exhibited joy in the discourses but were glad to be done with it. Ah,

---

34. SS 1:371-72.

but in those who preached with clarity what they did indeed believe, Spurgeon saw something entirely different. The old preachers, along with some of contemporary note, obsolete to the standard of the sophists, 'think the pulpit a throne, or a triumphal chariot, and are near heaven when helped to preach with power.' Including himself in the number, Spurgeon exulted, 'Poor fools that we are, preaching our "antiquated" gospel!' He enjoyed the task, for his 'gloomy doctrines' made him very happy. What a strange thing that what others considered 'very absurd and unphilosophical' was 'marrow and fatness' to him and 'do content us, and make us very confident and happy.' He had observed it in others also: 'I may say of some of my brethren, that their very eyes seem to sparkle, and their souls to glow, while enlarging upon free grace and dying love.'[35]

The joy of these truths, however, did not diminish the seriousness of the task. Just over three years before his death, Spurgeon preached on Malachi 1:1, focusing on the words, 'The burden of the word of the Lord' (NKJV). He knew well this burden and set forth the serious implications of this text for the preaching work of the pastor:

> The servants of God mean business. They do not play at preaching, but they plead with men. They do not talk for talk's sake; but they persuade for Jesus' sake. They are not sent into the world to tickle men's ears, nor to make a display of elocution, nor to quote poetry – theirs is an errand of life or death to immortal souls! They have something to say which so presses upon them that they must say it. 'Woe is unto me if I preach not the gospel!' They burn with an inward fire, and the flame must have vent. The Word of the Lord is as fire in their bones, consuming them; the truth of God presses them into its service, and they cannot escape from it; if, indeed, they are the servants of God, they must speak the things which they have seen and heard. The servants of God have no feathers in their caps – they have burdens on their hearts.[36]

---

35. *The Greatest Fight in the World,* p. 112.
36. SEE 12:263, 264.

5

'LET HIM MIND SOUL-WINNING'

. . . .

The initial impulse of evangelism

Among the first impulses of the recently converted Charles Spurgeon was to seek the salvation of his younger brother. He wrote his father, 'Oh, that the God of mercy would incline Archer's heart to Him, and make him a partaker of His grace! Ask him if he will believe me when I say that one drop of the pleasure of religion is worth ten thousand oceans of the pleasures of the unconverted, and then ask him if he is not willing to prove the fact by experience.'[1]

Spurgeon was conscious that this desire came along with the turning of his own heart to Christ. 'I think I never felt so much earnestness after the souls of my fellow-creatures as when I first loved the Saviour's name,' he recalled. He began the practice of writing verses of Scripture on slips of paper and dropping them along the way as he would walk to various destinations in Cambridge. He became part of a tract distribution society. He told his mother that he did not just hand a tract to the people on his route, but would sit down with them and go through the tract with them to help them understand it. Just three months after his conversion he wrote: 'I have most interesting and encouraging conversation with many of them. Oh, that I could see but one sinner constrained to come to Jesus.'[2] This remained the driving passion of his ministry. In an

---

1. Murray, *Letters,* to his father, 6 April 1850.
2. Murray, *Letters,* 24.

1862 sermon on 'The Sinner's End', he said, 'The burden of the Lord weighs down my soul this morning; my heart is filled even to bursting with an agony of desire that sinners may be saved! O Lord, make bare thine arm this day, even this day!'[3]

The Chief Calling and Dominant Commission

Spurgeon believed that the preeminent, no, the sole, commission of the Church, and therefore the preacher, was the call of winning souls. He warned his people against getting detoured into issues of less consequence than the eternal gospel and the destiny of souls. Hearing of the political influence of some ministers and admitting the subsidiary political impact of preaching, Spurgeon warned, 'But any Christian minister who thinks that he can do two things well, is mistaken! Let him mind soul-winning, and not turn a Christian Church into a political club ... our one business is soul-winning, our one banner is the Cross, our one Leader is the Crucified King!'

In like manner, Spurgeon spoke to his men at the Pastors' College. In a Friday lecture he stated: 'I purpose, if God shall enable me, to give you a short course of lectures under the general head of "The Soul Winner".' This was the foundation of his book by that title. He told them, 'Soul winning is the chief business of the Christian minister; indeed, it should be the main pursuit of every true believer.'[4]

Spurgeon's evangelistic ministry exhibited four characteristics fundamental to all that he did as a pastor: reflection on his experience of conversion, a sense of conscientious obedience, a strong theological commitment to the practice of evangelism, and an exploration of many avenues that might lead to engagement with needy sinners.

His Experience of Conversion

His conversion predisposed him to exhibit absolute dependence on the sovereign grace of God in evangelism. Spurgeon had reached

---

3. MTP 8:486: 'The Sinner's End.'
4. S&T, November 1879, front page.

a conviction early in his Christian life that the work of conversion was all of God. A journal of three months is larded with entries extolling the power and beauty of sovereign electing love.[5] He had unobstructed vision of 'the sparing mercies of the Lord'. This made him feel deep gratitude for 'His great grace in electing me, by the sovereign counsels of His love, to be one of His redeemed ones.'[6] Famously, he said, at sixteen years of age: 'Had the Lord not chosen me, I should not have chosen Him. Grace! Grace! Grace! 'Tis all of grace.'[7]

His Sense of Conscientious Obedience

Christ commanded the preaching of the gospel throughout the world, and the apostles went to the lost, preaching repentance toward God and faith in our Lord Jesus Christ. Spurgeon, contemplating the Great Commission, felt himself 'carried away by its power'. He could not 'calmly consider its terms'. He found it 'impossible to study' when 'thoughts were running here and there, asking a thousand questions.' How was he to go and follow each step of the commission from Jesus? The depth of this contemplation led Spurgeon to express his desire for the church to hear these living words of Christ addressed to her now: 'The injunctions of the Savior are perpetual in their obligation; they were not binding upon merely Apostles, but upon us also, and upon every Christian does this yoke fall.' We have no exemptions; prompt and perfect obedience is the only acceptable response. 'Brothers, the heathen are perishing; shall we let them perish? His name is blasphemed; shall we be quiet and still? The honor of Christ is cast into the dust, and His foes revile His Person and resist His Throne; shall we His soldiers allow this?' Skeptics and critics deny the possibility of the gospel's penetration into minds dominated by superstition and nations committed for generations to pagan religion. 'Shall we be content to foolishly sit

---

5. *Autobiography*, 1:125-43.
6. Ibid., 1:141.
7. Ibid., 1:134.

still? No, rather let us work out the problem; let us prove the Promise of God to be true; let us prove the words of Jesus to be words of soberness; let us show the efficacy of His blood, and the invincibility of His Spirit by going in the spirit of faith, teaching all nations, and winning them to the obedience of Christ our Lord!'

Spurgeon himself considered whether he should cast all aside and go to preach where none had preached before. He had made it a solemn question as to 'whether I might not testify in China or India to the Grace of Jesus, and in the sight of God I have answered it.' His position and responsibilities in England would not allow it, 'or else tomorrow I would offer myself as a missionary.' But were there not some who heard him who had gifts and zeal who would take that task as a personal call? Perhaps even now those who heard his voice also would hear the voice of thunder 'that as one man the entire Church might take the marching orders of her Lord, and go teach all nations, baptizing them in the name of Israel's God! O Lord, if we fail to speak, fail not thou to speak!'[8]

His Theological Commitment

Spurgeon was committed to a theology of means. If God saves, it will be in accordance with means. The angels sent to the elect man Lot 'did not omit a single exhortation or leave the work to itself, as though it were to be done by predestination apart from instrumentality.' The elect come when they are urged, persuaded, and entreated to look to the Crucified that they may be saved. Without dire constraint none will come. 'That constraint usually comes by instrumentality; let us seek to be such instruments.'[9]

Proclamation and exhortation are included, therefore, just as surely as incarnation and atonement, in the chain of means by which elect sinners are saved. 'Paul was cheered by the good news that God had many chosen and redeemed ones in Corinth whom He must

---

8. MTP 7:383: 'The Missionaries' Charge and Charta' (citation is p. 282, but see also p. 287).
9. MTP: 14: 'Lingerers Hastened.'

save,' Spurgeon explained. 'I learn from this,' he continued, 'that the doctrine of God's predestination is no check to labor.' Election does not repress zealous efforts at evangelism, but is 'the very thing that should awaken us to energy – that God has a people and that these people shall be brought in!' Earnest workers find encouragement in the doctrine of election, for it means that God 'will save and must save!' Go to work, therefore, 'under the sweet shadow of the Divine decree,' giving faithful witness to its energizing effect. 'It is a very sweet help to earnestness when we know that we shall not labor in vain, or spend our strength, and have no testimony to the saving beauty of redemption.'[10]

Spurgeon's caveat, however, leads to a consideration of three factors one must always bear in mind when engaging in evangelism. First, the faithful worker must always recognize the divine prerogative in granting of salvation. Often, the lost arrive at a place of deep conviction and yet find no peace of forgiveness and no sense of Christ's acceptance. 'It is one of the strange things in the dealings of Jesus,' Spurgeon wrote, 'that even when we arrive at this state of entire spiritual destitution', salvation may yet linger or not come at all.[11]

Spurgeon loathed the sinful pride that rejected divine sovereignty, that cavils at election, and makes accusations against God as prejudiced and partial. A person truly humbled by his sense of sin will not dispute the justice of God's condemning him or grumble against distinguishing grace. Jesus will have the sinner know that His gifts are in His own hand, totally within the pale of 'sovereign discriminating, electing grace'.[12]

A second factor concerns the Puritan idea of preparation. Delay in the immediate justification of the sinner has to do with the christocentric nature of conversion and the way of faith. Spurgeon, though modified in his preparationism, nevertheless believed that

---

10. MTP 26: 'Cheer for the Worker and Hope for London.'
11. *The Saint and His Saviour*, p. 102.
12. Ibid., p. 140.

sinners at times had to be taught to use the means of obtaining peace. They should hear sound gospel preaching, pray and call upon Christ, think of His promises, and meditate upon Him. Calls to believe without a clear perception of the object of faith are both vain and cruel. 'Faith,' Spurgeon argues, 'is a result of previous states of the mind, and flows from those antecedent conditions, but is not a position to which we can attain without passing through those other states.'[13]

Third, there are difficult places to labor and God might not always give to the laborer the effects of the light of the glory of God. Some places could be hard because they are under judicial blindness. A full submission to the divine will means that we will not always labor in propitious fields. Ezekiel must prophesy to dry bones and Jonah must go to hated Nineveh. God called them, and insisted on faithfulness. A task could appear impossible, but God's life-giving Spirit may act in accordance with a purpose to give life.[14]

Using a Variety of Means

Spurgeon engaged in evangelism through any means that he thought was warranted by Scripture or of which Scripture gave examples. Preaching in 1888, he lamented, 'I do not know what more I can do. I wish I knew; if there were any possibility of getting at some of you, to bring you to Christ, I would not leave a stone unturned.' The fullness of the Tabernacle always encouraged Spurgeon that at least some of the unconverted were hearing the proclamation of the Word. As long as God gathered the great crowd so that 'the most capacity of my voice is used up, this is the place for me to preach in.' Some people, however, will not attend such a place, so 'I must go to them'. Then, including the congregation in this urgent vision, he continued, 'We must take public calls and assembly rooms. We must even hire theaters and music halls, or stand in the streets – we must speak to the people.'[15]

13. Ibid., p. 157.
14. MTP 47: 'Christian Resignation.'
15. MTP 34: 'The Charge of the Angel,' www.spurgeongems.org.

Out of Doors

The history of the Church taught him the fruitfulness of evangelism in the open fields. As a young minister, he yearned for itinerancy. If he could not itinerate, he could not bear to preach. Remaining in one place, he protested, would make the preacher indolent and the people indifferent. Gospel-hardened ground is hard to plow. Among his chief ambitions, while still holding forth regularly in his own pulpit, was to traverse the entire land. He believed that itinerancy is God's great plan, for God's elect are scattered throughout.[16]

Early in his ministry he reported an outdoor service in Hackney where he preached to 10,000; in this event he had 'climbed to the summit of a minister's glory'. Profound silence reigned during the message; after its close 'never did mortal man receive a more enthusiastic ovation!' He had to be borne away from the crowd, waving his hat as he went, in a commandeered carriage. The wave of his hat was returned by thousands.[17]

On the Streets

Spurgeon practiced and encouraged evangelism on the streets. His church members and his students received instruction and admonition to be seriously involved in reaching the dirty, unwashed, miserable, unchurched throngs of London's Southwark. His art at this is described in an article entitled 'Spurgeon among the Costermongers'. People accused him of building a church on the 'rabble' of London. Who needs the gospel more than the rabble? The most desperate, bloated, wicked, demoniacal, and vile must be gathered from the highways and hedges.[18]

He told his congregation on the second Sunday of 1868 that every believer should be an ambassador from heaven by being faithful in intentional evangelistic efforts. No idle hands, but 'both

16. SS 1:337.
17. *Letters*, 'To Susannah Thompson,' 2 June 1855 and 23rd of the same month.
18. SS 1:304.

hands occupied in leading souls to Jesus Christ'. He rejoiced in those who labored, but others 'do but very little for my Lord and Master'. While London is perishing, and multiplied thousands presently are sinking down where neither tears nor prayer can reach them, 'You let them go as though it were of no consequence,' he urged; 'you utter no lamentation, and make no efforts on their behalf.' As he viewed the urgency with which the angels brought forth Lot from Sodom, he pled: 'Let the text rebuke you, my fellow-labourers, and God give you grace to be more earnest in future.'[19]

For some, Spurgeon warned, a punctilious sense of separation and unwarranted moralism would keep them from going to sinners in their habitat. You must never say: 'I cannot talk to these people, they are so depraved and debased; I cannot enter that haunt of sin to tell of Jesus.' Carriers of the gospel should be angels of mercy where demons destroy. The woman who is a sinner must receive kindness, 'for Jesus looked on her with mercy.' With Jesus as exemplar, no type of sin in all its terrible connotations is to be beneath pity nor beyond labour. Those who have wandered farthest, firebrands already smoking, must be snatched from the fire.[20]

Twenty years later, Spurgeon still pressed his people on. Searching for souls was not easy, especially in London, for the native depravity of man had been further degraded in hardness by the vicious life so easily followed and so oppressively dominant. It is easier to find pearls in the bottom of the sea than to seek for souls in wicked London. If God's presence and promise were not with them, their eyes would go blind and their tongues would wear thin before they would find any to grasp Christ as a Redeemer. But presence and promise press the seeker of souls forward, and he will bring with him the 'chosen of the Lord'. As a church, they were the Bridegroom's friends and they would 'sigh and cry till we have found the chosen hearts in whom He will delight'.[21]

---

19. MTP 14: 'Lingerers Hastened.'
20. Ibid.
21. SS 19:352.

Benevolence

The benevolent organizations in the Tabernacle were mainly for evangelistic purposes. Spurgeon saw these as giving completion to the gospel in its effects on the converted. Surely if we know the love of God, we will express love to men. If we have seen from the heart the greatest commandment, to love God with all of our being, then the lesser commandment will follow in its natural course. Though these benevolent organizations were good in and of themselves, Spurgeon always saw personally, and emphasized publicly, that their roots not only were embedded in gospel compassion but were for the purpose of gospel proclamation.

The large number of relief efforts, targeting different groups in different places, put the ministry of the church in the hardest and neediest places of London. None in the congregation had an excuse for doing nothing. If they could not preach on the corners of the busy London Streets or in the gruesome and crowded districts of poverty and vice, then surely they could collect socks, shoes, clothes, food, and give them to the needy along with a gospel tract written by Spurgeon himself. Spurgeon often commented on the Tabernacle being as busy as a beehive with some useful organization meeting each day of the week preparing for benevolent outreach for the sake of the gospel.

The Church exists to hold forth truth, righteousness, compassion, and selflessness in its zeal for the glory of God while it retains a deep conviction of the spirituality of its aims. A London church that does not do good 'in the slums, and dens, and kennels of the city is a church that has no reason to justify its existence any longer!' Heathenism must be reclaimed, evil must be fought, error must be destroyed, and falsehood put down; 'a church that does not exist to take the side of the poor, to denounce injustice, and to hold up righteousness, is a church that has no right to be!' As Christ laid aside His glory for others, the glory of the church emerges most purely 'when she lays aside her respectability and her dignity, and counts it to be her glory to gather together the outcasts, and her highest honor to seek amid the foulest mire the priceless jewels for which Jesus shed His blood!' Her heavenly occupation is to 'rescue souls from hell, and lead them to God, to hope, to heaven.'[22]

Thus he pursued the well-being and just treatment of the poor as an absolute good in itself but as subservient to the ultimate importance of eternal and spiritual matters. Spurgeon insisted that 'the church will do well when she remembers that she wrestles not with flesh and blood ... but with spiritual wickedness.' She dispenses not the 'law and order by which magistrates may be upheld, or tyrannies pulled down'; instead her good transcends the temporal, while affecting the temporal. She wields a 'spiritual government by which hearts are conquered to Christ, and judgments are brought into subjection to His truth.' Under the authority of the dying Christ, the Church is to strain after the forgiveness of sinners, warn against sin, point to the eternal remedy in the blood of Christ, be clear on the consequence of hell for unforgiven sin, and the glory of heaven for those forgiven. 'The more she keeps to this, the better.'[23]

He taught and tooled his church to take its share in battling the evils that afflict humanity. They, and he, worked for temperance, education, political reforms as time and energy allowed. The first business, however, is with 'the hearts and consciences of men as they stand before the everlasting God'. This, he constantly pronounced, 'is your one business; tell sinners that sin will damn them; that Christ, alone, can take away sins, and make this the one passion of your souls.'[24]

The Preeminence of Doctrinal Preaching

The Tabernacle Pulpit, accordingly, was an evangelistic Pulpit. As he engaged in a description of the terror and fright of the day of judgment in which the lost would sing a 'chorus of unutterable woe, ... wherein he will have to growl, and howl, and sigh, and

22. SEE 4:311. MTP 15: 'The First Cry From the Cross.'
23. Ibid.
24. SEE 4:312.

cry, and moan, and groan forever,' one of the potentially damned interrupts: 'And can you leave me without telling me what I must do to be saved?' Spurgeon responded, 'I trust not; I hope I shall never preach a sermon without speaking to the ungodly, for O! how I love them.'[25]

Spurgeon's sermons, therefore, filled with doctrine, always had an evangelistic application since he first preached at Waterbeach.[26] When he heard of the first convert from his preaching at Waterbeach, he went to visit her and later wrote: 'Then could I have sung the song of the Virgin Mary, for my soul did magnify the Lord for remembering my low estate, and giving me the great honour to do a work for which all generations should call me blessed, for so I counted and still count the conversion of one soul.' More highly to be valued was the winning of a soul 'from going down to the pit' than any honor of politics, any degree in academic theology, any accolades of oratorical skill, or any ecclesiastical honor.[27]

Not only was doctrinal preaching evangelistically informed, all true evangelistic preaching is full of doctrine. 'The sermons that are most likely to convert people,' Spurgeon lectured, 'are full of truth: truth about the fall, truth about the law, truth about human

---

25. SS 2:186.
26. See Christian George, Ed. *The Lost Sermons of C. H. Spurgeon: His Earliest Outlines and Sermons Between 1851 and 1854* (Nashville: B &H, 2016), p. 165, sermon outline 19. Based on 2 Samuel 24:13 and entitled 'An Answer Required', Spurgeon focused exclusively on the gospel that requires an answer. After giving several ways in which the gospel comes through its messengers, and several wrong attitudes and answers, he concluded by giving exposition of the correct answer, 'I accept it,' and added the exclamation, 'O that some may say so. Amen.' Also see p. 435. In sermon outline 71 entitled, 'What Think Ye of Christ?', he spoke of the inadequacy of the answer given by the heathen, Jews, 'the Mahometan and Mormonite,' atheists, deists, Arians, and Socinians. The first point emphasized that our answer to the question will affect 'Our Closing with the Gospel'. For another intensely doctrinal and evangelistic sermon, see p. 322 ff, 'He Took Not Up Angels,' based on Hebrews 2:16. In closing, Spurgeon said, 'Yet God, to manifest the sovereignty of His grace, chose man. Learn hence the justice of election as well as its grace' (p. 324).
27. Ibid., 1:199.

nature, and its alienation from God, truth about Jesus Christ, truth about the Holy Spirit, truth about the Everlasting Father, truth about the new birth, truth about obedience to God, and how we learn it, and all such great verities.'[28] Even when he preached with the greatest clarity and fervor the great doctrines of sovereign grace and the sinner's absolute dependence on the eternal decrees of God, Spurgeon insisted that every person must know that there is no doctrine of Scripture that discourages a sinner from coming to Christ, nor any doctrine that excuses a sinner from faith in Christ and love to Him.

Spurgeon often began his sermons announcing his prayer that someone would be saved through the message. In the beginning of a sermon on Lot's escape from Sodom he told the congregation his intent. 'I thought, this morning, that perhaps the Lord might make me to some of you the angel of mercy by enabling me to lead you out of the Sodom of your sins and to conduct you into a state of present salvation. Oh, how I long for this with eagerness of desire!'[29] On 19 April 1868, a sermon on 'Bringing the King back' issued this prospect at the start: 'I shall endeavor to speak pointedly, and may the Holy Spirit make an effectual application of each word. May I but win a throne for Jesus in any one heart, and my joy shall be full.'[30]

Virtually all sermons have an earnest evangelistic component to them. Even those that are most polemical have as their concern the lack of any saving truth in the perversions of the gospel. His sermons on purely Calvinistic themes are applied in ways to give the evangelistic emphasis. A sermon on the atonement promised, no matter a person's present condition, 'No man ever perished who from his heart rested in the atoning blood.'[31] A sermon on the 'Mission of the Son of Man', defended particular atonement and

---

28. *The Soul Winner*, 1895, p. 90f.
29. MTP 14:789: 'Lingerers Hastened.'
30. MTP 14:808: 'Bringing the King Back.'
31. MTP 21:1251: 'The Sacred Love-Token.'

included an encouraging word to those convinced of their lostness: 'It is a good thing to be so lost; it is a happy thing to be lost to self, and lost to pride, and lost to carnal hope. Christ will save you. Believe that. Look to Him as He hangs upon His cross. One look shall give you comfort. Turn your weeping eyes to Him as He bleeds there in misery. He can, He will save you.'[32]

Spurgeon encouraged witnesses thoughtfully and prudently to introduce poor souls 'to the deeper truths of our theology'. It is better to learn them early and hear them from 'loving, tender-hearted Christians, than from hard, careless loveless spirits'. Embarrassment about God's revelation is a poor way to introduce Him as a trustworthy Savior; 'it is poor policy to try and conceal truth. It has a little of a Jesuitical look about it.' If we are ashamed of the doctrine of election, 'let us revise our creed; but in the name of common honesty let us hide nothing which we believe. The more light the better.' Doctrine in its full truthfulness and in all its biblical connections had been the source of his soul's health and joy from his youth and would be still in his old age. 'So far from being ashamed of the Election of Grace, it commands the enthusiasm of my whole being.'[33]

How should seekers respond when they hear the doctrine of election? Taking his cue from the Canaanite woman of Matthew 15, Spurgeon pointed to her words, 'Lord, help me,' and encouraged, 'My dear hearer, do that, and do it *now*. No doctrine will trouble you long: I am sure it will not.' The doctrine of providence does not cause any to cease from attending to daily business. In the soul's business, one may let the Lord do what He will, but the cry of the soul still must be, 'Lord, help me.' A soul in distress comes 'wholly submissive, but heartily adoring.' Such who come feel that 'the divine Saviour must and will save every soul that hangs upon Him'. Spurgeon assured his hearers, particularly those under the weight of afflicted consciences, that 'there never was a soul' and

---

32. SS 6:107, 108.
33. MTP 30:1797: 'How to meet the Doctrine of Election'; SEE 7:35

there 'never can be a such a soul' that 'came to Christ and Christ did cast it away'. Souls are not drawn apart from divine intention and a sense of desperation and danger. Those who will yield, who come to Him and trust Him, will 'rejoice that the lines of electing love have encompassed you'.[34]

The evangelistic power and intent of doctrine entered at the front of Spurgeon's sermons, made their way through the varied explanations and perorations, and gave purpose and point to the end. Spurgeon always tied the character of the appeal to the doctrinal gravity of the sermon, but even in isolation from the body of explanation, his search for souls is unmistakable. As illustrations of the multiplicity of such evangelistic calls, these two show the intensity of his earnestness. 'From my soul I pity you who do not know what the love of Christ means. ... Depend upon the merit of His sacrifice; cast yourselves entirely upon that, and you are saved, and Christ is yours.'[35] 'Cry mightily unto the Lord for salvation, and trust alone in the Lord Jesus. He will save you. If you were between the jaws of hell, yet, if you believed in Him, He would surely pluck you out of destruction. God grant you may find it so, for Christ's sake.'[36] All who had longings for reconciliation could come with the confident assurance that 'He will in no wise cast out'.[37]

As he closed a special service for young people of the church, based on Psalm 2, he reminded them that God deals with us only through His Son. He is God with all His power and perfections, and He is man with all our duties for righteousness and unblemished worship. In Him alone, therefore, is to be found the perfect righteousness as well as the expiatory sacrifice for sin that all sinners, even the nice children of church members, need. He alone is the needed advocate. They should seek no works righteousness, nor think that faith is a means to be saved from the sorrow of the world. No. They need

34. SEE 7:43, 44.
35. SEE 9:41. From a sermon, 'The Believer Not an Orphan.'
36. MTP 21:1253: 'The Lion-slayer – the Giant-killer.'
37. SEE 9:320.

to escape from the freshly-kindled anger of the Son. 'Kiss the Son then,' he urged. Filled with affection, but no platitudes, with the love of a father or brother above the *ex officio* duties of a preacher, he repeated, 'Kiss the Son *now*. Yield your heart up to Jesus now. Blessed are they that trust in Him right now.'[38]

Evangelistic Literature

Spurgeon produced literature designed to be used for evangelism. In his first book, *The Saint and His Saviour*, Spurgeon ended each of its twelve chapters with a postscript entitled 'To the Unconverted Reader.' In the second of the twelve, Spurgeon reflected on how the wounds of conviction that come to the converted should affect the unbeliever. 'Thou thinkest it a blessing to be free from the sad feelings we have been describing, but let me tell thee it is thy curse.' As he developed that thought, he brought it to maturity in saying, 'Theirs is a hopeful distress; thine will be a hopeless agony. Their chastisement comes from a loving Jesus; thine will proceed from an angry God. Theirs has for its certain end eternal salvation; thine everlasting damnation.' As he concluded in following through with this theme, Spurgeon wrote: 'Why then despise those whom grace has turned, and who therefore are constrained to bid thee turn from the error of thy sinful ways? May the Lord stay thy madness in time, and give thee repentance.' He ended by saying, quoting Isaiah 30:33, 'otherwise, "Tophet is ordained of old: the pile thereof is fire and much wood; the breath of the Lord, like a stream of brimstone, doth kindle it".'[39]

All of Grace contains short expositions of the doctrine of grace. It begins with the words, 'The object of this book is the salvation of the reader. He who spoke and wrote it will be greatly disappointed if it does not lead many to the Lord Jesus. It is sent forth in childlike dependence upon the power of God the Holy Ghost, to use it in the conversion of millions, if so He pleases.' The final chapter is a

---

38. SS 12:86-107.
39. *The Saint and His Saviour*, pp. 98-100.

closing appeal of four deeply personal and winsome pages. The last paragraph begins with the urgency present throughout: 'Reader, meet me in heaven! Do not go down to hell. There is no coming back again from that abode of misery. Why do you wish to enter the way of death when heaven's gate is open before you? Do not refuse the free pardon, the full salvation which Jesus grants to all who trust Him.'

In the preface to *The King's Highway*, Spurgeon defended the sermons, not as technically accurate works of literary art, but as consistent with orthodox theology and proven effective as useful for conversion. 'No new gospel have we aimed to declare,' Spurgeon confessed. Not a new creed but more faith, not another covenant but greater confidence – those are the great needs of the hour. 'Our colours are nailed to the mast, and in doctrine we take for our motto, *Semper idem*.' To those who would find this approach contemptible, Spurgeon pointed triumphantly and defiantly to this fact: 'There is scarce a sermon here which has not been stamped by the hand of the Almighty, by the conversion of a soul.' Some, particularly 'None But Jesus,' had been abundantly blessed in that way.[40]

Personal Evangelism

Spurgeon believed that the practice of personal evangelism was a 'holy art'. He knew Christians 'who can go up to individuals and talk to them with freedom about their souls', but he found this difficult personally. He worked at conquering the hesitation. When he did so, he found large reward. He admired the humble Christian who prays for both souls and opportunities and is enabled to 'address a loving word to sinners'. The best tools of soul-winning, so Spurgeon observed, are the 'emotion we feel and the affection we bear'. The Holy Spirit uses tender hearts to break hard hearts.

Frequently called on to give help to souls by way of written correspondence, he gave himself to the privilege in earnest. In a

---

40. *The King's Highway*, pp. 6, 7.

letter to William Cooper, in 1851 when Spurgeon was seventeen, he began with an honest warning about what was at stake in coming to Christ. 'If you give yourself time to think, you will soon remember that you must die; and if you meditate one more moment, you will recollect that you have a soul, and that soul will never die, but will live forever; and if you die in your present state, it must live in endless torment.' 'There is no way of salvation but Christ,' and none but He can do any sinner good. But He is indeed the helper of the helpless and 'I tell you that He died for all such as feel their vileness, and come to Him for cleansing.' Properly to grasp the value of Christ's death one must know and feel that 'there is not a jot of merit on the sinner's part mentioned in the covenant.' The sinner is nothing and has nothing to bring, 'but Christ is all, and He must be everything to you, or you will never be saved.' The only way to heaven is by faith, in itself a gift of God – 'Oh may you possess it! is the earnest prayer of ... Charles H. Spurgeon.'[41]

During his first months as Pastor in London, he received a letter from T. W. Medhurst asking Spurgeon to be candid enough to inform his tortured soul 'whether there is any hope that I belong to the elect family of God; whether Jesus Christ His Son has ever died for me.' Spurgeon expressed his gratitude for Medhurst's expression of feeling such driving concern for this question. At present, however, it is a question 'neither you nor I can answer'. Other questions must come first. In the Puritan fashion of preparationism, Spurgeon pressed Medhurst with the question of his knowledge of his sin and of the true nature of belief. He reminded him of the certainty of hell for unbelievers and that salvation 'must be entirely by unmerited mercy'. Should he grasp with heart clarity the severity of his sin, then the advice would be, 'Believe on the Lord Jesus.' But, though awakened, he probably does not understand what true belief is. He advised him, therefore, 'seriously to be much alone,' to 'let your groans go up if you cannot pray,' and 'attend as many services as

---

41. *Letters*, pp. 67-69.

possible'. If he seeks in earnest, faith will come soon. Catching himself, as if he were advising something short of the immediate responsibility to believe, he wrote, 'But why not believe now? You have only to believe that Jesus is able and willing to save, and then trust yourself to Him.'[42]

Special Meetings

Spurgeon taught his church to see itself as an evangelistic organism with many members, each part doing that which it is gifted to do. No one does everything, no one does nothing, and everyone has a particular assignment from the Lord in the business of calling out His people. On one occasion, he used a Monday evening Lord's Supper as an evangelistic opportunity, when 1,500 met to receive the Supper and 1,000 sat in the galleries to observe. Following that, about 200 met with the officers of the church, who at Spurgeon's request issued brief but earnest and poignant exhortations to believe in the crucified Savior. Sixty persons remained after the meeting, and, so the report asserted, 'there is every reason to believe many were saved by the blood of Christ applied to their consciences.'

He held special evangelistic meetings at the church, often using those within the church who were gifted at evangelism, teaching, and manifested a consistency in earnestness about souls. Obviously these were selected very carefully. These meetings always involved a week of preparatory prayer meetings. Then meetings with special groups, young people, children of deacons and elders, and others, were interspersed through the week. Other targeted groups on a larger scale met throughout the week for very pointed and purposeful presentations of the gospel.

He trained a group of counselors for these meetings. No less than a quarter of an hour must be spent with each enquirer, but often twice to three times that much is required. This is necessary to form any estimate of the spiritual condition of the person and

---

42. *Letters*, pp. 69, 70.

render efficient aid. In the evening more enquirers came and were faithfully dealt with by some of the elders and 'other friends'. These 'other friends' were specially selected by the pastor for this purpose. He held prayer meetings with them and gave training for the most effective help throughout the time of meetings.

More than thirty large volumes containing 15,000 testimonies written by these counselors are presently housed in the Metropolitan Tabernacle. They bear testimony to the effectiveness of this careful training of counselors and the serious sense of gospel stewardship that they maintained. One example of these 15,000 testimonies may be seen in the case of Amy Mawby. H. B. Hackett wrote the account. His first entry said: 'Has been seeking Jesus for some time – was brought up to the Church of England and has greatly displeased her Father and Mother by not attending (as they call it) her church.' Further down the page, Thomas Moor wrote: 'She called again this evening but I am not at all satisfied with her testimony; I told her to continue attending Mrs Bartlett's class, and see Bro. Hackett again.' Finally, Hackett wrote: 'I have seen this young friend several times during the last six months. At first I recommended her to Mrs Bartlett's class, she has been regular in her attendance since last April. She is now rejoicing in Christ and I had much pleasure in giving her a card.'[43]

Thomas Moor, who coordinated with Hackett above, interviewed twenty-nine-year-old James Boyce, a careless, gambling, drinking ne'er-do-well who had observed a communion service at New Park Street, came under conviction within days, and was converted. Moor wrote: 'He is another of the many wonders of sovereign grace, another witness to the power of the Holy Spirit to subdue the rebellious, another testimony to the greatness of that love, which out of the black depths of fallen humanity bringeth forth those who, being made white in the blood of the Lamb, become pillars in the living temple of the living God.'[44]

---

43. Personal photo of handwritten note in Enquirers Book for 9 and 16 April 1862, in archives of the Metropolitan Tabernacle.
44. Wyncoll, pp. 39, 40.

Seeking True Revival

Throughout his ministry, Spurgeon maintained resolute caution about revival meetings and the use of evangelists. In 1866, Spurgeon warned that 'vital godliness is not revived in Christians by mere excitement, by crowded meetings, by the stamping of the foot, or the knocking of the pulpit cushion, or the delirious bawlings of ignorant zeal.' Such stock-in-trade techniques of revivalists may excite yet-dead souls but for the sake of living souls 'we must go directly to the Holy Ghost for it, and not resort to the machinery of the professional revival-maker'.[45] Because revivalists omitted the truth that salvation delivers 'from the power as well as from the guilt of sin', Spurgeon pointed to the 'fervent revivalist' as having injected a teaching that could do as much hurt as good.[46]

Nevertheless, Spurgeon did not rule out in principle that God still gave some to be evangelists. An 1891 report for the Pastors' College that included 'The Pastors' College Society of Evangelists,' also contained an *apologia* by W. Y. Fullerton for the effectiveness of itinerant evangelism and its usefulness for the Church. Spurgeon, due to the influence of a friendship with D. L. Moody, had become persuaded 'of the great value of the office and work of evangelists'. Spurgeon participated in Moody campaigns and had Moody preach at the Metropolitan Tabernacle. When Moody was in Scotland in 1874, Spurgeon gave eight pages to a report of its phenomena, saying that Moody 'has the resolute faith of a true apostle'.

Accordingly, Spurgeon determined to sponsor evangelists through the College in 1877. He personally engaged to find them maintenance that 'they may go through the length and breadth of the land and preach Christ'.[47] The first two were A. J. Clarke, the preacher, and Manton Smith, the singer and horn player. He sent them on their first assignment in August 1877. Clarke was a humble

---

45. S&T, 1866, p. 532. The article was entitled 'What Is a Revival?'
46. MTP 17:979: 'Faith and Regeneration.'
47. S&T, 1877, p. 334.

Christian and displayed great natural gifts in preaching. Spurgeon gave Manton Smith a 'new silver trumpet, upon which is engraved a verse from the Psalms, "With trumpet and sound of cornet, make a joyful noise before the Lord and King."' Both evangelists had been useful in conversion work and they were sent forth in the name of the Lord 'with high hopes of blessing'.[48]

Conceding the validity of itinerant evangelists, and even fully engaged in their support and sponsorship, Spurgeon nevertheless wanted due caution in an area so fraught with the possibility of charlatanism and emotional abuse. In his 1879 lecture on soul-winning, Spurgeon warned that 'soul-winning is not accomplished by hurriedly inscribing more names on our church role, in order to show a good increase by the end of the year.' He had seen many a person made worse, turned into hypocrites, made an embarrassment to the church by unwise zeal. 'Undue pressure, well-meant but ill-judged,' in an overzealous attempt to get decisions is not evangelism. Reports from the field of conversions during a single night's work of immediate harvesting sounded hollow, and dangerously deceitful, to Spurgeon. He was weary of the 'counting of unhatched chickens, this exhibition of doubtful spoils.' One should hope for the best but in the time of highest excitement still should be reasonable. 'Enquiry rooms are all very well, but if they lead to idle boastings they will grieve the Holy Spirit and work abounding evil.'[49]

Spurgeon had idealized the First Great Awakening in America and the ministry of Jonathan Edwards. In 1880, he stated his desire to be a part of 'a revival like that under Jonathan Edwards in which there were no extravagances, no utterances of false doctrine, no making a noise and a riot – but just the preaching of the old-fashioned Doctrines of Grace!' He expressed a sincere desire 'to see that old kind of work and life among us again!' Spurgeon would not dictate to the Holy Spirit what He must do, but contrasted Edwards'

---

48. Ibid.
49. S&T, 1879:505.

awakening with contemporary revivalists and asked rhetorically, 'Nowadays – where are the converts of your revivals?'[50]

Resurging Anglican sacramentalism alarmed Spurgeon of its subtle development within evangelicalism. He feared that modern revival techniques could introduce an incipient sacramentalism. Reflecting, in 1883, on the regularity of conversions in his preaching services, combined with the care to avoid such Romish superstition, Spurgeon observed with cautious satisfaction: 'Those converted under our ministry are seldom of the "after-meeting kind," excited, and over-persuaded.' Instead, they would go their way, think the matter over, and if the true work of the Spirit was present, profess their faith when 'they have tried themselves, and tested their conversion.'[51] Even as late in his ministry as 1890, Spurgeon advised: 'There are little things among ourselves which must be carefully looked after, or we shall have a leaven of ritualism and priesthood working in our measures of meal.' He warned against the notion that in the inquiry room something may be gained which is not to be had at once in the assembly. To come back virtually to a trust in altars and confessionals in this manner is only a coarser form of 'Romish trumpery'. 'If we make men think that conversation with ourselves or with our helpers is essential to their faith in Christ, we are taking the direct line for priestcraft.'[52]

Still in 1891, Spurgeon wanted to distinguish between revival and revivalist technique. 'Some misunderstood me the other day to speak against revivals,' he marveled. 'I never did such a thing in my life! The more revivals we have of a true sort, the better.' What he spoke against was the method of incitement that pumps people up, lets them drop, and leaves them as hard as nails. He did not want 'spasms of any sort'. A temporary ripple on the surface would not do, 'but a great swell that comes rolling up from the depths! May God send it!'

---

50. MTP 26:1566: 'Cheer for the Worker and Hope for London.'
51. S&T, 1883:562.
52. S&T, 1890:262.

Finally

Spurgeon rejoiced that through the years of his ministry 'souls have been saved in one continued stream by the preaching of the Gospel'. He awaited, however, with positive expectation 'for a grand spring tide, a mighty flood that shall bring many to Christ and to the Church! Then it shall be that God will get to Himself a glorious and an everlasting name!'[53]

---

53. MTP 37:2229: 'God's Glorious and Everlasting Name.'

6

'EXTREMELY UNWELL AND
EXCEEDINGLY DEPRESSED'

· ·

Spurgeon contemplated the effects of conversion on his love for
the Bible. Before it had fascinated him as a book of grandeur,
charm and wonder, but he did not gain the benefit of its spiritual
power. It also had been a book of great terror; and had it not been
mixed with ever-alluring hope of salvation by calling on the name
of the Lord, Spurgeon confessed that he would have been 'driven to
the commission of suicide through grief and sorrow'.[1]

When he was converted, however, the 'inner meaning shone
forth with wondrous glory', and he accepted it with no hesitation
as the unerring oracle of God. It was the source of intense joy for
him. 'From that hour,' he testified, 'I bless God, that being not
exempt from trouble, and especially not free from a tendency to
despondency which is always with me, I yet rejoice and will rejoice,
and am happy, unspeakably happy in resting upon Jesus Christ.'[2]

Spurgeon learned to identify, among the many avenues through
which distress could come, two types. 'An affliction that will talk
is always a light one,' he surmised, for one can discern its purpose
and its benefits. 'But I dread most of all a dumb affliction, that

---

1. *Autobiography*, 1:75.
2. Ibid., 1:107.

cannot tell me why it has come.' The tried one cannot find God, walks in a maze, does not know what to do; he must live solely on the knowledge of God's wisdom and goodness, and cherish Job's confidence: 'When He hath tried me, I shall come forth as gold.'[3]

In a letter to young people, written near the end of his life, Spurgeon remarked, 'In times of deep depression – and I have had plenty of them – I have feared this and feared the other, but I have never had any suspicion of the goodness of my Master, the truth of his teaching, or the excellence of his service.'[4]

By his own testimony, we see that Spurgeon had a 'tendency to despondency' that remained with him throughout life. At the same time, he found revealed truth as a more powerful molder of mind. The pleasure of the Bible was an abiding source of tonic against depression for Spurgeon. In 1869, he revisited the text of his first sermon, 1 Peter 2:7, and began with a frank confession followed by an immediate remedy: 'My brethren, I am quite out of order for addressing you tonight. I feel extremely unwell, excessively heavy and exceedingly depressed, and yet I could not deny myself the pleasure of trying to say a few words to you.'[5] The Bible, especially its witness to the preciousness of Christ to the believer, pleasured him even in the throes of depression.

The strength of divine grace empowering divine truth pressed him beyond his dark propensity and moved him beyond the slippery downward spiral constantly lurking beneath his emotions. On 19 February 1850, he wrote his mother that he had 'been in the miry Slough of Despond'. He told her that his grandfather had sought to bolster his spirits, 'but is that what I want? Ought I not rather to be reproved for my deadness and coldness?' He prayed, heard, and read

---

3. SEE 14:427, 428.

4. Spurgeon, *A Good Start*, pp. 61, 62. The book was first published in 1898 as a collection of articles and letters written by Spurgeon largely for encouraging young Christians to serve with energy and faithfulness and for the lost to trust in Christ.

5. SEE 2:81.

without doing any of them heartily but in 'deadness and coldness'. When he recovered from this bout with despondency, he described the extreme depth of it, as well as the remedy to escape it, a remedy that remained with him through his ministry: 'In the blackest darkness I resolved that, if I never had another ray of comfort, and even if I was everlastingly lost, yet I would love Jesus, and endeavor to run in the way of His commandments: from the time that I was enabled thus to resolve, all these clouds have fled.'[6]

The Great Calamity: Fake Fire in Surrey Gardens

God Prepared Him

In 1856, prior to the panic at the Surrey Gardens Music Hall, Spurgeon preached on Elihu's words in Job 35:10: 'But none saith, "Where is God my Maker, who giveth songs in the night?"' (KJV). The distress and great sorrow that overwhelm many Christians arise when 'they are looking about, on the right hand and on the left, to see how they may escape their troubles,' but forget to look to the One from whom all true help comes. Calling to mind God's mercies from eternity past to the blessed hope, Spurgeon emphasized that the eternal electing purpose of God should give a song to a Christian even in his deepest sorrow. He must remember his conversion and his rescue from the chains of sin and coming wrath. Such a memory of present blessing should make song rise from his lips. He can rejoice in like blessings in the lives of others. The Christian should learn to sing of such mercies at all times. By so doing, a company will arise cheered by the song of confidence and faith. 'Sing! Perhaps you will get a good companion by it. Sing! Perhaps there will be many a heart cheered by your song. There is some broken spirit, it may be, that will be bound up by your sonnets. Sing!'[7]

It was good that Spurgeon had these thoughts as ballast for his soul, for he soon would need to find a song in the night.

---

6. Murray, *Letters*, to his mother, 19 February 1850.
7. SS 2:183.

From Worship to Woe

19 October, Sunday evening. Thousands of people were gathering, pressing into the Hall, ascending steps, squeezing into seats, and anticipating the engaging style, the Gospel-centeredness, and the marvelous voice of the preacher. When the event was contemplated, some of the faithful resisted the idea as soiling the event of preaching in a place designed for worldly entertainment; others dismissed the relevance of the venue but embraced the opportunity for around 12,000 people to gather to hear the gospel. Three galleries and the floor were filled, pressed together.

Scripture-reading, a hymn and a prayer – and at the prayer's opening a cry from one part of the building and then repeated in other parts: 'Fire! The galleries are giving way!' This occurred in the farthest reaches of the great hall. Spurgeon knew that something had caused confusion, but those nearer the pulpit yelled 'Preach!' He preached, with awareness that a false alarm had been sounded, and warned against the real and final alarm of judgment. The sermon was short, his concern was real, and the remaining congregation sang, 'His sovereign power without our aid,' and then left orderly and quietly.

Only after the service did Spurgeon learn of seven deaths and numerous serious injuries. He was so distraught that his deacons sent him away into the country. The daily papers used the event to evoke 'for Mr Spurgeon and his rantings the profoundest contempt'.

And Back Again – God Restored Him

Preaching at New Park Street Chapel on Sunday evening, 2 November 1856, Spurgeon examined the text from Psalm 22:1: 'My God, My God, why have You forsaken Me? Why are You so far from helping Me, and from the words of My groaning?' (NKJV). This was his first evening message after the fatal calamity at the Surrey Gardens Music Hall that sent him into an almost suicidal distress. He posed the biblical query, 'Why are You so far from the words of My roaring?' As he contemplated that Christ Himself released the 'deep, solemn groan which is caused by serious sickness and which suffering men utter', Spurgeon observed: 'Beloved, many of us can sympathize with Christ, here. How often have we, on our knees, asked some favor of God and we thought we asked in faith, yet it never came?'

In his commentary on the Psalms, Spurgeon likened this to 'the roarings of a wounded animal'. Continued prayer and continued divine silence, bended knees and brass heavens, gave eruption to the question, 'Can there be a God?' Christ's words became his, 'My God, my God, why have You forsaken me? Why are You so far from the words of my roaring?' Is this like God to appear silent, to refuse to answer when one knocks, to seem unkind, to spurn the sinner, to ignore His promise? Through our experience with God at times we may reflect this, but certainly not to the degree and for the purpose expressed in the cry of Jesus. 'Yet there was a reason for all this,' Spurgeon commented on Psalm 22, 'which those who rest in Jesus as their Substitute well know.'

Two months after that sermon, Spurgeon penned a preface to the second volume of his *New Park Street Pulpit*: 'Ebenezer! Hitherto the Lord hath helped me. Truly may this writer say this. In fact, he is compelled, before he proceeds to write a few words of preface, to express his hearty thanks that he is able to write at all. Great and sore troubles have rolled over his head; he has been exceedingly cast down.' After a time of a 'mournful song' he entered a season of 'merciful restoration', in which 'renewed health and vigor demand new exertion and fresh gratitude'.[8]

God Taught Him

This message on Psalm 22 led to an event that Spurgeon shared in another sermon some years later (1881) as he preached out of Ezekiel 40. Ezekiel had been for fourteen years in captivity and needed to see something of the wisdom and purpose of God. 'God's children are brought in experience to unusual places, on purpose, that they

---

8. SS 2:v (preface).

may get clearer sights of the love and Grace and mercy of God in Christ than they could obtain elsewhere.' Spurgeon shared that on some occasions (not always), God showed him for what purpose he had been in a state of distress. He reminded the congregation of the Psalm 22 sermon preached twenty-five years earlier. 'If ever a minister preached from that text fearing that it was true of himself I did! I was under an awful darkness all the while and I could not tell why.'

The following evening, however, during his weekly reception of enquirers, he talked with a man who seemed 'not far from madness'. Spurgeon must have been puzzled to see this man whose eyes were staring from his head and whose face was full of terror. 'You have delivered me from self-destruction,' he said. Feeling that he was forsaken of God, no one ever had spoken in a way that touched his soul or entered into his experience until he heard Spurgeon's sermon on the previous evening. 'By God's great Grace and infinite bounty,' Spurgeon continued, 'we were able to pilot that Brother into smoother waters and I hope that he now lives to rejoice in God.' At that point, Spurgeon, in his words, 'felt thankful to the last degree that I had been dragged through all my depression because I was able to help him.'[9]

At another place in the Ezekiel sermon, Spurgeon mused: 'Whenever you have much joy, be cautious – there is a sorrow on the road. But when you have much sadness, be hopeful – there is a joy on the way to you – you can be sure of that.' God reveals Himself to His distressed people 'more in the valleys, in the shades, in the deeps than He does anywhere else, ... making the darkness light by His Presence. Saints have seen Jesus more often on the bed of pain than in robust health.'

As he progressed in his analysis of God's ministry to Ezekiel, Spurgeon's reflections again uncovered the deep of his own journey in pain. Promises need 'dark soul-trouble' in order for the brightness of their meaning to take root. 'Much of faith's education may be called black-letter learning. Very black the letters are, too, and very

---

9. MTP 27:1578: 'Taught That We May Teach.' www.spurgeongems.org

ugly looking, and they must be peered over.' Many promises do not yield their profundity 'till you are in the dark and when the soul is in gloom'. This is the Lord's doing to press His children to 'gaze upon the starry promises and value every ray of light that streams from them'. In this way, sufferers 'may be prepared to see bright visions of Himself and know Him better, love Him better and serve Him better.'

As we move to the end of Spurgeon's ministry, in 1891, still we find that this sense of abandonment experienced after the Surrey Music Hall tragedy informed his morphology of the spiritual dark night giving way to the morning sun of grace. A summary of his point is made clear in aphoristic style: 'If the Holy Spirit glorifies Christ, that is the cure for every kind of sorrow.' He then reminded them of what he had shared before, that after the 'terrible tragedy in the Surrey Gardens, I had to go away into the country and keep quite still.' Even the sight of a Bible made him cry, for he 'was heavy and sad, for people had been killed and there I was, half dead, myself.' The thought that brought him back, however, was based on Philippians 2 and Acts 5:31: 'Him hath God exalted with His right hand to be a Prince and a Savior' (KJV). Spurgeon saw himself as a common soldier left to die in a ditch who would raise himself up on an elbow and express his love and fealty to the prince as He rode by, for He was emblazoned on his heart. A consciousness of the exaltation of Christ provided the cure for every spiritual malaise. That earlier crisis was only a species of the crisis he felt in the holy war of the Downgrade, and Spurgeon found the answer to such distress constant: 'If our Lord and King is exalted, then let other things go which way they like. If He is exalted, never mind what becomes of us.'[10]

Theologian of Suffering

Even in the intensity, longevity, and befuddlement that characterized Spurgeon's pain, he never lost sight of the reality that it served a theological purpose. He wanted others to see it in that light also.

---

10. MTP 37:2213: 'Honey in the Mouth!' www.spurgeongems.org

So strongly did he believe that suffering was within the purpose of the covenant of redemption, that he considered questioning the wisdom, faithfulness, and purpose of God in suffering and death to be a 'vile argument'. Preaching on the raising of Lazarus, and reflecting on Martha's proposition, 'If you had been here,' Spurgeon answered: 'It is Christ's love that has suffered you to be despised and down-trodden. It is Christ's love that has let you remain in affliction, because the divine benefit that has come of it is more to your profit than the thing itself could ever be to your loss.' What advantages, therefore, did Spurgeon find in suffering?

Relation of Suffering to Sin

Spurgeon considered all kinds of sickness and sorrow as the result of sin. 'In consequence of sin we have become sick and infirm and liable to suffer.'[11] These came on the heels of the fall of 'our first parents', and might not be the immediate result of one's personal sin, but they certainly flow from the full corruption of nature, affections, conscience, and body that stemmed from Adam's fatal disobedience.

In 1857, Spurgeon published *The Saint and His Saviour,* in which there is a chapter entitled 'The Causes of Apparent Desertion'. With great sensitivity, Spurgeon drew on his knowledge of Scripture set in the context of both pre-conversion and post-conversion experiences. 'He casts the Christian down,' Spurgeon taught, and 'gives the most afflictions to the most pious'. One might even say that God makes 'more waves of trouble roll over the breast of the most sanctified Christian than over the heart of any other man living.' This world is not the place of punishment, but punishment and reward are in 'the world to come'. The only reason, then, why God afflicts His people must be this:

> In love I correct thee,
> thy gold to refine,
> To make thee at length
> in my likeness to shine.[12]

---

11. *The Gospel for the People,* p. 434.
12. SS 4:333-34. NPSP 1857, p. 453.

The sanctifying influence of suffering creates tenderness toward others, an enlarged sense of dependence on God, a more hopeful longing for heaven and the immediate presence of Christ, and a greater sense of the union of justice and mercy in personal afflictions.

Suffering and Sympathy

Preaching on a Sunday evening in the Metropolitan Tabernacle, Spurgeon reflected on the event recorded in Matthew 8:16, 17 where Jesus healed 'all that were sick' and cast out demons in fulfillment of Isaiah's prophecy, 'Himself took our infirmities, and bare out sicknesses.' As he reasoned from the lesser to the greater, Spurgeon revealed how his own tendency to despondency gave him both empathy and increased distress in counseling the emotionally downtrodden. He found that when he entered into one 'sorrowful case after another' that he was 'more sad than any of them'. He worked to share their trouble so that he could speak with sincerity, but found that nothing 'wears the soul down so fast as the outflow of sincere sympathy with the sorrowing, desponding, depressed ones.' Though he found that he often had been helpful to others at such times, the help 'has cost me dearly'. 'Hours after,' Spurgeon confessed, 'I have been myself depressed, and I have felt an inability to shake it off.'[13]

If identification with the sufferings of others afflicts us in such ways, how much must the sinless Son of God have suffered in sorrow of soul as He took the full weight of our sin to Himself, and suffered the full measure of payment for them. 'Sin is the root of our infirmities and diseases; and so in taking the root, He took all the bitter fruit which that root did bear.'

Though Spurgeon indicated a high degree of personal assurance of salvation with few if any abatements, his struggles with despondency made him sensitive to those who might also have issues with such assurance. Preaching in Exeter Hall in 1861, he frankly told the large

---

13. *The Gospel for the People*, p. 433.

crowd from all over London: 'I must confess here, with sorrow, that I have seasons of despondency and depression of spirit, which I trust none of you are called to suffer, and at such times I have doubted my interest in Christ, my calling, my election, my perseverance, my Saviour's blood, and my Father's love.' On this occasion, he did not defend either his doubts or his having shared the experience. In fact, since he was preaching on the absolute trustworthiness of 'The Glorious Right Hand of the Lord', he confessed that he had sinned both in his doubts and in his sharing of them publicly. 'I feel I have no excuse to offer either to him or to you for having dared to doubt him. 'Twas a wicked sin.' He did not want his weakness, and his failure to be an example of strong faith, to produce a puny Christianity unable to sustain the battle with fierce and unwavering trust in a faithful God.[14]

Nevertheless, he would have other occasions both of distress and public confession of it. He had to learn to negotiate between the strength and certainty of the decree and acts of God on the one hand, and the weakness of redeemed humans struggling with both finitude and indwelling sin on the other. Preaching in 1887 on 'The Child of Light Walking in Darkness', Spurgeon fully sympathized with those who experienced periods of dark foreboding concerning their spiritual state. 'Let it be clearly known that some of us,' speaking autobiographically, 'who even this day speak with fully assured confidence, have in days gone by, been sorely shaken, and have cried unto the Lord out of the low dungeon.' Shifting to a more clearly personal testimony, he continued: 'Every particle of the faith which I have this day in the Lord my God has passed through fire, and through water.' Though presently he exhibited a 'flaming torch of confidence', its brightness and heat 'was lighted for me when I was in darkness'. He was sure that 'at some time or other, all the children of God walk in darkness.'[15]

---

14. MTP 7:363: 'The Glorious Right Hand of the Lord.'
15. SS 18:357.

In the hymnbook he edited for his church, *Our Own Hymnbook,* he included a section on 'Holy Anxiety'. Hymns by Samuel Davies, William Cowper, Samuel Stennet, Benjamin Beddome, Isaac Watts, Henry Bateman and Philip Doddridge are included. A verse from Davies on 'self-examination' makes the request:

> Searcher of hearts, oh search me still,
> The secrets of my soul reveal:
> My fears remove; let me appear
> To God, and my own conscience, clear!

From Cowper we would be led to sing (or perhaps only meditate silently):

> Oh, make this heart rejoice or ache!
> Decide this doubt for me;
> And, if it be not broken, break,
> And heal it, if it be.

Benjamin Beddome would lead the worshipper to examine the heart with perfect candor and then call on the God of grace to intervene:

> What crowds of evil thoughts,
> What vile affections there!
> Envy and pride, deceit and guile,
> Distrust and slavish fear.
>
> Almighty King of saints,
> These tyrant lusts subdue;
> Drive the old serpent from his seat,
> And all my powers renew.

On 2 March 1890, Spurgeon returned to the text of Psalm 22:1, but this time from its gospel fulfillment in Matthew 27:46: 'My God, my God, why have you forsaken me?' Less than two years from his own death and with the Downgrade two and a half years old, he felt some personal identification with the reality of physical distress combined with mental fatigue and spiritual desertion. Again, he saw in the substitutionary death of Christ the balm for weary souls and wounded spirits. 'Grief of mind is harder to bear than pain of body,' he reflected. 'You can pluck up courage and endure the pang of sickness and pain so long as the spirit is hale and brave. But if the soul itself is touched and the mind becomes diseased with anguish, then every pain is increased in severity and there is nothing with which to sustain it.' But descending from mental sorrow to spiritual sorrows is a journey into even deeper distress: 'A man may bear great depression of spirit about worldly matters if he feels that he has his God to go to.' But if he feels that the Lord is withdrawn, and His presence is shadowed even for an hour, 'there is a torment within the breast which I can only liken to the prelude of Hell. This is the greatest of all weights that can press upon the heart.'[16] Spurgeon's comments on the Psalms lead frequently to autobiographical consideration on the many lamentations contained in them. He believed that part of God's giving fitness to him as a minister of the gospel was bound up in a fitness to understand the torturous pain and distress of both spiritual and physical suffering. How could he understand Scripture and how could he be a tender shepherd to his people if he were not a fellow to the infirmities and sorrows so abundantly displayed in the Bible?

On Psalm 88, commenting on verse 6, 'Thou hast laid me in the lowest pit, in darkness, in the deeps' (KJV), he searched this language and considered the condition of the writer: 'It is grievous to the good man to see the Lord whom he loves laying him in the sepulcher of despondency; piling nightshade upon him, putting out all his candles, and heaping over him solid masses of sorrow.' As he considered that principle in the lives of other biblical characters he gave the note of encouragement that 'God never placed a Joseph in a pit without drawing him out again to fill a throne; that He never caused a horror of great darkness to fall upon an Abraham without revealing His covenant to him; and never cast even a Jonah into the

---

16. MTP 36:2133: 'My God, My God, Why Have You Forsaken Me?' www. spurgeongems.org.

deeps without preparing the means to land him safely on dry land.' Then he turned to his own struggles with these pits of darkness and confessed: 'He who now feebly expounds these words knows within himself more than he would care or dare to tell of the abysses of inward anguish. He has sailed round the Cape of Storms, and has drifted along by the dreary headlands of despair.'

He moved then to a statement of general consideration and closed with a christological application. 'Those who know the bitterness by experience will sympathise,' Spurgeon continued, 'but from others it would be idle to expect pity, nor would their pity be worth the having if it could be obtained.' God ordained 'bitterness of experience' for Spurgeon so that he might sympathize. Another, however, knows these pains to an infinite degree, far outstripping the sense of abandonment ever experienced by any mortal: 'It is unspeakable consolation that our Lord Jesus knows this experience, right well, having, with the exception of the sin of it, felt it all and more than all in Gethsemane when he was exceeding sorrowful even unto death.' Spurgeon made use of his depressions of spirit to gain insight into similar wars in the soul that he found in the pages of Holy Scripture.[17]

Deal Gently

Spurgeon knew that there were Christians who thought that depression was an evidence of faithlessness. 'There are some special, superfine, hot-pressed Christians about nowadays who ... say "You ought to be joyous; you ought never to be depressed; you ought to be perfect."' Perhaps so, Spurgeon meditated, but warned also that they may find some day 'that it is more difficult than they think, as some of us have sometimes done.'[18]

When Spurgeon preached on the interaction that Jesus had with the thief on the cross, he used it as an opportunity to illustrate how tenderly we must deal with those in despair. The man saw that Jesus

---

17. *The Treasury of David*, 2:4.
18. SEE 14:427. This is from a sermon entitled 'Believers Tested by Trials'.

was in the same place he was, but undeservedly so. He also had heard Him call God His Father and pray for His tormenters. 'And so the Light of God came to the dying man who had been so long in the dark!' Jesus' treatment of this man became a paradigm for how we treat the suffering and depressed. 'I hope, Brothers and Sisters, that you will never get down so low as that, but I beseech you, if you ever meet with any others who are there, do not be rough with them.' Some are likely to be hard on those who are depressed in spirit and seek to shake them out of it by reprimand and even harshness. 'Really, you ought to rouse yourself out of such a state,' they might say. Then he personalized the state of the downcast ones: 'I hope none of you will ever have such an experience of this depression of spirit as I have had – yet I have learned from it to be very tender with all fellow sufferers.' Jesus, however, reaches down in tender mercy to rescue those who stand in the Slough of Despond, for 'if He does not, they will sink in deep mire where there is no standing.'[19]

The disciples on the road to Emmaus were allowed to tell their whole story of confusion when Jesus approached them. 'Do not talk too much yourselves,' Spurgeon observed, but 'let the swelling heart relieve itself.' Those who seek the Lord must be able to tell their difficulties and 'do not discourse much with them until they have done so'. Deep sorrow often is silent and must find a tongue before it can receive words of cheer and encouragement. Sometimes, because misery thrives on mystery, an unfettered encouragement to describe the disease of sorrow will in itself effect the cure. Sometimes, one may extract the mystery by description and 'the sharpness of the woe is over'.[20]

In Spurgeon's final sermon in the Metropolitan Tabernacle, preached on 7 June 1891, he discussed 'The Statute of David for the Sharing of the Spoil'. To Spurgeon, this event showed that 'Some saints are constitutionally depressed and sad'. He noted further, 'They

---

19. SEE 4:323. MTP 48:2803. 'The Saddest Cry from the Cross' was preached in January 1877, but it was not published in the MTP until 1902.
20. SS 18:304.

are like certain lovely ferns which grow best under a constant drip.' The Lord will gather to Himself these lovely ferns of the shade 'as well as the roses of the sun!' They will find Him attentive to them as much as the sunflowers and 'the saddest shall rejoice with the gladdest'.

Drawing on Bunyan's images, Spurgeon called on the Little-Faiths, Despondencies, Much-Afraids, and Feeble-Minds who 'sigh more than you sing', who have a 'great heart for holiness but feel beaten back in your struggles', to be heartened at the Lord's munificence in giving them their part of the spoils of salvation. David, the indefatigable warrior-king, was determined to share the spoil even with those who were unable to go with him for the rescue of their families and their goods. Though partially at fault in their shy insecurities, Spurgeon took cue from David and assured them that 'your infirmities shall not be reckoned as iniquities! If lawfully detained from the field of active labor, this statute stands fast forever, for you as well as for others – "As his part is that goes down to the battle, so shall his part be that tarries by the stuff: they shall part alike."'

The Necessity of Suffering

Spurgeon believed that suffering was necessary for confirmation of the Christian in orthodoxy. 'Some men want a sound pummeling with affliction to get them to love Christ,' Spurgeon asserted; 'And some old professors need a touch of poverty, sometimes, or a little affliction, or a rack of rheumatism and that brings them to their bearings and they begin to cry out after realities and get rid of whims and fancies!' When confronted with all the pressures of doctrinal divergence that ridiculed substitutionary atonement, Spurgeon proclaimed that 'the Cross is the school of orthodoxy'.

He found it to be so with himself. He recalled 'quiet moments at Mentone' when he had such a sense of the divine presence and redemptive provision that he wished for wings of a dove to fly him to England to speak to his people in that moment of orthodox exhilaration. 'I have been very sick and full of pain and depressed in spirit and I have judged myself to be, of all men, most unworthy and I judged truly.' Then without losing the sense of unworthiness, or rather gaining a keener sense of his worthiness of hell, 'then it was that my Substitute was my hope and in my lonely chamber at Mentone I clung to His dear garment! I looked into His wounds! I trusted myself with Him, again, and I know that I am a saved man!' Jesus in His person and work is unique and salvation can be in no other. 'You will not be led away to any other doctrine' in such moments of despair.

Spurgeon found that in 'close dealings between God and your soul – and death stares you in the face – nothing will do but a crucified Redeemer.' From where can confidence come in such a state but from 'a sinner's childlike reliance upon the finished work of Him who suffered in our place?' Spurgeon knew that his words which placed suffering as an encouragement to orthodoxy were strong, but he confessed, 'I feel a thousand times more strongly than I can speak.'[21]

On another occasion, Spurgeon referred to this benefit of suffering as making the sufferer 'an established Christian'. We need not a bulrush faith that bows to the wind but one 'rooted and grounded in assurance of faith'. When the clouds and darkness make one go to God, he discovers that a 'tried faith' grows into a 'strong faith' and that faith 'ripens into full assurance'. God gives us treasures in the darkness and turns our mourning into dancing.[22]

Suffering is Necessary for Chastening

At the celebration of Spurgeon's twenty-fifth anniversary as pastor in London, he told his people, 'During the time that I have been preaching the gospel in this place, I have suffered many times from severe sickness and frightful mental depression, sinking almost to despair.' The constant strain had made it necessary for him to be 'laid aside for a season' each year. So deep had the difficulty been at

21. MTP 26:1546: 'Men Bewitched.'
22. SS 18:369.

times, that he asked for patience if future years showed even more wear and tear. He would be at his post when he could, but if he became too ill, he hoped that 'I shall have the grace to be the first to perceive the fact and shall be ready at once to leave the position to an abler occupant.' Given even that reflection on the severity of his trials, yet he could say, 'I believe that affliction was necessary to me and has answered salutary ends.'[23]

In 'Twelve Covenant Mercies,' preached on 30 June 1889, Spurgeon talked about 'needful chastisement', citing Psalm 89:30 in support. God never will remove His everlasting love or fail in faithfulness, yet to deal with transgression in the believer 'the rod shall be sure to fall upon you, and sometimes its strokes shall come upon you before you transgress, to keep you from sinning.'[24] He learned of the great suffering of one of God's dearest servants, a prosperous man who used his wealth discreetly and wisely. When a sharp and heart-breaking affliction came on him, Spurgeon said to himself, 'Yes, yes, God loves him; God loves him.' The man himself would testify that 'he has not all sweets to drink, to make him sick and ill; but there are bitter tonics, sharp blows of the rod, to keep him right.' That we have not escaped the rod should be substance for praise. 'Sickness is a choice blessing from God; I cannot measure the unutterable good that comes to us full often in that way.' Other trials, including losses in business, bereavements, and depressions of spirit, 'are all, when we see them in the light eternal, so many covenant mercies.'

Spurgeon had suffered for so long, with such intensity, and in both physical and mental ways, that he had learned to discern peculiar blessings from God through the avenue of suffering. He questioned, therefore, the wisdom of those who would resort to 'faith healers' in order to sidestep pain as quickly as possible. 'Do you not think that we all make mistakes as to what will be a blessing?' he proposed. 'In

---

23. LeVos, 48.
24. SEE 5:506.

the matter of faith-healing,' he continued, 'health is set before us as if it were the great thing to be desired above all other things.' But is this really so, he questioned. 'I venture to say,' he answered, 'that the greatest earthly blessing that God can give to any of us is health, *with the exception of sickness*. Sickness has frequently been of more use to the saints of God than health has.' Obviously with specific cases in mind, Spurgeon opined, 'If some men, that I know of, could only be favoured with a month of rheumatism, it would, by God's grace, mellow them marvelously.' Possibly in the chamber of suffering they would find new insights into divine grace and provision and have 'something better to preach than what they now give their people'. He wished for no one a long time of sickness and pain, 'but a twist now and then one might almost ask for him.' Trials – 'a sick wife, a newly made grave, poverty, slander, sinking of spirit' – give lessons to be learned in no other context, and drive one to 'the realities of religion'. Chaff may work for nutrition when one has no real work to do, but when there is pain to endure, grief to bear, and pastoral sympathy to give in good earnest, the old corn of the land is what you want, 'and you must have it, or else you will faint and fail.'[25]

On a Monday evening of the first week after the congregation began to meet again there, subsequent to a renovation of the building, Spurgeon pondered the severe work of tearing out, scraping, gouging, and ripping up that preceded the restoration of soundness and beauty in the Tabernacle.[26] In this he saw an analogy to how God uses affliction of various sorts to sanctify His people. 'The pools of the heart are apt to grow stagnant unless stirred by affliction.' An undisturbed life becomes a hotbed for 'shams and superficialities'. We should thank God for sending sharp troubles, keen temptations, and rough providences. They will strip away what is rotten and leave what is real and lasting. Such trials 'lay bare the poverty and nakedness of our natural estate', and like a

---

25. *An All Round Ministry*, p. 384f.
26. S&T, 1867: 266-67.

careful auditor 'finds out the bad debts, the risky speculations, the worthless paper, the spurious securities which the soul has been dealing in, and sets our spiritual efforts upon a less cheering, but more certain footing.' Thus, the painful work of truth prepares us 'for manifestations of the Lord Jesus' sweetest love'. Spurgeon had found in his own sufferings that 'it is only as we are brought low in self, that we are lifted up in the ways of the Lord. A harshfaced providence has proved itself to be a good friend.' He welcomed the hand 'which covers me with wounds and bruises, and so leads me to seek the Physician of my soul.'

Suffering Produces Refined Joy

Spurgeon did not forget that the Bible speaks of 'various trials' and being 'tested by fire' in the context of 'joy inexpressible and full of glory' (1 Pet. 1:6-9 NKJV). When, therefore, in 1874 he strongly recommended cheerfulness as an evidence of true faith and a necessary tool for witnessing, it was in the context of a carefully-considered grasp of the source of cheerfulness. 'I commend cheerfulness to all who would win souls,' Spurgeon wrote. This virtue was not the superficial contrived 'levity of frothiness', but a sincerely 'genial, happy spirit'. If we want people to go to heaven with us, then we must surmise that 'there will be more souls led to heaven by a man who wears heaven in his face, than by one who bears Tartarus on his looks.'[27]

Reflecting on the tradition of the royal horses wearing bells as they pulled the royal carriage, Spurgeon determined that, in his service for his eternal King, bells should inform people of the royal nature of his task. Cheerfulness, the bells that adorn a forgiven sinner, gives maximum effectiveness to the Christian's witness for Christ. 'I am bound to see to it that the royal horses shall not lack for bells.' Seeking to do holy work with 'depressed spirits and gloomy views is as difficult as for the artist to paint with worn-out brushes'.

---

27. S&T, 1874.

Cheerfulness helps a Christian care for his tools. It 'sharpens the edge, and removes the rust from the mind. A joyous heart supplies oil to our inward machinery, and makes the whole of our powers work with ease and efficiency.' We must take special care, therefore, to maintain a 'contented, cheerful, genial disposition.'

Spurgeon suspected that the 'deadening gloom and murderous chilliness of certain religionists' made them guilty of the blood of souls. Who wants a relationship that produces no joy, nothing about which to smile, and nothing that produces expressions of cheer? People shun moroseness as they shun the death-damps of malarious swamps. Christians should be happy, for 'they serve a happy God'. Reflecting on the biblical witness to the infinite and eternal blessedness of God, Spurgeon noted that 'It enters into the essential idea of God that he is superlatively blessed. We cannot conceive of a God who should be infinitely miserable.' How contradictory therefore that, if the Christian pilgrimage makes one more like God, we should instead become more and more miserable. 'It would be a singular and unaccountable thing indeed, if, by acting like the Giver of all good, whose bliss is perfect, we should increase in wretchedness.'

This does not mean, however, that the bells indicate life is free of trial. On the contrary, Spurgeon pointed out, 'It must be so.' When the gold knows the purpose of the fire, who stoked it, and that refinement and greater value is at the end of the process, it will find 'a sweet satisfaction even in the flames'. The godly thank the Refiner for the process and for watching over it with such perfectly-tuned skill and benevolent determination. 'A sad heart goes mourning to its loneliness, sullenly murmuring at its hard lot, but the stout heart repairs to the throne of grace, and opens its mouth wide that God may fill it.'[28]

Suffering Presents Death as a Friend

During the winter of 1885, Spurgeon underwent one of his most severe experiences of pain combined with melancholy. As he tried

---

28. S&T, 1866:98, 100.

to write the preface to the 1885 bound volume of the *Sword and the Trowel,* he explained, 'I am utterly hard up.' Readers should not expect much scintillating insight from his pen: 'Every limb of my body is tormented with pain; there is about as much pain in each limb as any one of them can conveniently bear.' More distressingly, the mind-body unit was in a state of 'fidgets, *malaise,* and depression.' Could someone be chained in his place he would gladly yield, but since none is handy, 'we must tug the oar even if we snap our bones.' He managed two paragraphs, then down with the pen. 'A hurricane, consisting of rushes of pain, twitches, and all sorts of deadly apprehensions' assaulted him. Later he completed his duty-bound preface only by dictating to an amanuensis.[29]

Writing around the same time as he composed the notes of the January 1886 *Sword and Trowel,* he reported that 'Brain weariness has driven the Pastor to take his accustomed rest.' The delay in going brought on the painful attack, which was caused not so much by the recurrence of his disease, as by 'general weariness'. On 17 December, he described a 'balmy day of clear sunshine and summer warmth' in Mentone. He could sit outside all day and drink in the healing influences of sun, sea, and air. 'There is nothing like it for an invalid, to whom the cold and the damp are killing.' He hoped soon to be on his feet, with a refreshed brain ready for full work again.[30]

When he addressed the College Conference in May 1886 he was in great pain and had had to miss the greater part of the Conference. During his inaugural address his pain made it hard to think and 'almost impossible to think connectedly'. Almost all that he had prepared was forgotten and 'no new springs of thought could make channels for themselves while the mind was smothered up in physical suffering.' He hesitated to prepare the message for publication in the magazine, but friends reminded him that *The Sword and the Trowel* was largely autobiographical and it should certainly appear

---

29. S&T, 1885, Preface.
30. S&T, 1886:42.

as the testimony of a man who could 'with difficulty keep himself from tears through acute suffering and yet was resolved to take his part in a meeting which he had anticipated with solemn interest for months before.'

Later in 1886, Spurgeon preached from Job's words: 'For I know that thou wilt bring me to death, and to the house appointed for all living.' He reasoned with his congregation that death was not a bitter contemplation but, to those that were great sufferers, quite relieving. 'I have on several occasions felt everything like a fear of dying taken from me simply by the process of weariness; for I could not wish to live any longer in such pain as I then endured.' If so vivid with him, Spurgeon reasoned 'that such an experience is common among sufferers from acute disorders'. He was not surprised by the phenomenon of suicide, but was surprised that it was not more frequent, for he testified concerning himself, 'I could readily enough laid violent hands upon myself, to escape from my misery.' He had observed that great sufferers 'would sooner rest from so stern a struggle than continue the fierce conflict'.[31]

For the Christian, however, suicide was not the answer to suffering, nor was suffering designed to provoke attempts at suicide. Rather, pain is designed to give an increased hope in Christ, a more consistent and intense desire to be in His presence, and great courage and even satisfaction in the face of death. Spurgeon preached, 'Those who die daily will die easily,' and reminded his congregation that 'Those who make themselves familiar with the tomb will find it transfigured into a bed: the charnel will become a couch.' Pain as a precursor of death reminds those who rejoice in the covenant of grace 'that even death itself is comprehended among the things which belong to the believer'.

Spurgeon invited those who heard him to learn this lesson of pain and then to transform their view of death. He wanted them

---

31. SEE 6:152; For a more extended discussion of this, see Zack Eswine, *Spurgeon's Sorrows*, pp. 119-31.

'to look this home-going in the face until you change your thought and see no more in it of gloom and dread, but a very heaven of hope and glory.' We live as dying men among dying men but have a perspective that encourages us to meditate on it rather than put it aside as something we never intend to use. This meditation 'will not make us unhappy', for the hope of heaven is not expressed in a desire 'to live here for ever'. If pain robs us of comfort here, and gives a sense of doom to this life, we will conclude that 'it were a sad sentence if we were bound over to dwell in this poor world for ever'. No, we will grow ripe and be carried home; we will labor to the end and go home and 'receive the wares of grace'.

Among the greatest escapes presented by heaven was 'no more depression of spirits'. In the present, however, pain, sickness, and distress serve to give a deeper desire for heaven. 'Is there anything dark and dismal about that?'

7

'HE KEEPS TALKING ALL
ABOUT HIMSELF'

· ·

'I hope you will forgive me for taking up so much space about myself;
but at present my thoughts are most about it.'[1] This caveat, in a letter
to his father in the first month of 1850, came after a written stream of
conscientious analysis of mixed gratitude and fear – gratitude for saving
grace and the hope of eternal life, and fear that he might dishonor the
gospel by personal neglect. Later, writing to his uncle in November
1850 having used the word 'my' eighteen times, he caught himself and
confessed, 'He keeps talking all about himself.' He continued, 'True,
he does; he cannot help it,' adding, 'Self is too much his master.' 'I am
proud of my own ignorance; and, like a toad, bloated with my own
venomous pride, proud of what I have not got, and boasting when I
should be bemoaning.'[2] Whether sinful or mere spiritual transparency,
one must become accustomed to Spurgeon's reflections on personal
experience and his tendency to universalize it for others.

Difficult Necessity of Self-Knowledge

For the reality of self-knowledge, Spurgeon pointed to his own
times of reflection on the deeply-seated ambivalence that seemed

---

1. Murray, *Letters,* p. 20.
2. *Autobiography,* 1:193. Also in *Letters of C. H. Spurgeon.* A letter to his uncle,
   November 1850.

to dominate every aspect of being. 'If any man thinks that he knows himself thoroughly,' he instructed, 'he deceives himself; for the most difficult book you will ever read is your own heart.' In counseling a doubter, whose spiritual journey was in a maze, Spurgeon observed, 'Well, really I cannot understand you; but I am not vexed, for I never could understand myself.' This was an earnest moment of counseling encouragement and was a key to his vigorous commitment to self-analysis as paradigmatic to all human experience. 'Watch the twists and turns and singularities of your own mind, and the strangeness of your own experience,' he advised. Each person should examine his depravity of heart alongside the work of divine grace; the tendency to sin as well as the capacity for holiness; he should observe his 'kinship to a devil, but also how allied to God Himself.' Next to a thorough knowledge of biblical doctrine, Spurgeon saw a knowledge of one's own heart 'to be of immense importance to you as a watcher over the souls of others'. This is the 'laboratory in which he tests the medicines which he prescribes for others'.[3]

Spurgeon joined the company of Martin Luther who opined that 'the experience of the minister is the best book in his library'. Spurgeon was persuaded that God 'leads His servants through peculiar states of mind', not only for themselves but for 'those to whom they may afterwards minister'. Spurgeon narrated a time of coldness in his devotion when he found no ground in his heart for 'comfortable assurance' of being a recipient of saving grace. His feelings toward the Father as well as his love and gratitude towards Jesus Christ for His redemption were cold and 'almost extinct'. His heart was like an Arctic sea of ice and not like 'the crystal lake which is ruffled with every passing breath of the breeze'. His heart sank. But into his mind this thought flashed – 'The Holy Spirit can produce within your heart all those emotions you are seeking for, all those desires you gladly would feel, all the melting, and the

---

3. *Lectures*, 1:198.

moving, and the yearning, and the rejoicing, which are significant of the Grace of God.' In a moment his callous sensibilities were driven away, and he was 'filled with adoring love'. He marveled that God should condescend to work with such gross material and groveling minds. Not only could spiritual life and its joy be restored but they could also be sustained safely into the eternal kingdom. The revival of love and felt trust made him 'eager for prayer, and my joy and peace in believing were more than restored to me.' Then he reasoned that others were 'in a similar case, and especially there may be seeking souls who, seeing what must be worked in them before they can hope to be partakers of the eternal rest, may despair that such a work should ever be done.' They may feel hopeless. 'Perhaps,' Spurgeon thought, 'if I remind them that "The Spirit also helps our infirmities," that Jesus Christ's bequest to us, in virtue of His having gone to Heaven, is an Omnipotent One,' their hearts might be encouraged and they would be enabled 'to look with restful confidence to Him who works all our works in us'.[4] He was afflicted that he might comfort others.

Discernment of True Conversion

This self-study would shape Spurgeon's approach to his membership interviews as he sought to discern the depth and pattern of others' professions of faith. '"Now, sit down," I say sometimes, when I am seeing an enquirer or a candidate for church-membership, "and I will tell you what were my feelings when I first sought and found the Saviour."' Often the seeker would exclaim, 'Why, sir! that is just how I have felt; but I did not think anyone else had ever gone over the same path that I have trodden.' If we fail to probe the way others have experienced grace, we perceive our path a solitary one; but he who increases in knowledge of God's striving with others 'is well aware that their experiences are, in the main, very much alike.'[5]

---

4. MTP 18:1045: 'Joy in a Reconciled God.'
5. *Lectures*, 2:139.

Given his commitment to his conversion as a paradigm, he trusted that he could lead interviewees into a path of experience that would engage them with sympathetic feelings. He could help with the words and the images and they would provide the affirmation. So many times had he rehearsed the windings of his soul in the five-year struggle toward finding a merciful Christ, that he could engage the enquirer at any stage of his spiritual journey and duplicate the succession and level of emotion and the moment of repentance and faith. He wanted to discern the way in which God's Spirit dealt with people and to show them the analogy of experience that existed throughout the whole company of the redeemed.

Just barely veiled, he used his own testimony as an example of the Word coming with power. 'Those who are really God's elect,' he intoned, 'can tell a tale something like this.' He imaged the Word, in the coming of the law as a ten-thonged whip that stripped bare the seeker's shoulders and gashed his soul. In such a condition, he would realize his debt to justice and that God was against him. He was shamefully stripped naked and 'leprous from head to foot'. He was 'bankrupt and a felon' ripe for a 'traitor's doom'. Spurgeon continued, imposing his experience on that of the enquirer, 'Truly the Word came with power to your soul.' Then Spurgeon personated the earnest enquirer assuming his language, 'I remember too when the truth came home to my heart, and made me leap for very joy, for it took all my load away; it showed me Christ's power to save. I had known the truth before, but now I felt it.' These truths were formerly understood in the head but now gripped his heart. 'I went to Jesus just as I was,' would be the words of the new convert; 'I touched the hem of his garment; I was made whole. I found now that the Word was not a fiction – that it was the one reality.' Such a person can say, 'I had listened scores of times, and he that spake was as one that played a tune upon an instrument; but now he seemed to be dealing with me, putting his hand right into my heart, and getting hold of me.' In summary, when the truth comes crashing home in a saving manner, the seeker would say, 'He brought me first to God's judgment-seat, and there I stood and heard the thunders roll; then He brought me to the mercy-seat, and I saw the blood sprinkled on it, and I went home triumphing because sin was washed away.' Spurgeon then gave the final thrust, 'Oh, I ask you, did the Word ever come home with this power to your souls?'[6]

Another element of his own struggle to salvation was the deep sense of hopelessness. On occasion he would probe the experience of another using the sense of abandonment as a canon of investigation and counsel. 'Do you not recollect when you felt it to be so?' he asked. 'When sin lay heavily upon your conscience, Satan came and wrote over the lintel of your door, "NO HOPE," and the grim sentence would have stood there to this day had not a loving hand taken the hyssop and, by a sprinkling of precious blood, removed the black inscription.' Without hope and without God – that such a condition should change is a true marvel, 'that assurance should have taken the place of despair!' As unregenerate persons, we – Spurgeon linked himself with the newly-graced sinner – pursued false hopes and fell into 'bogs of presumption and error. – we had no hope.' No storm is so dreadful and terrible as the words 'No hope'. Yet into that thick darkness we continued, seeking reliance on 'good works, outward ceremonies and good resolutions.' 'No Hope' resounded with dread monotony, until we wished for death. Now, however, though no less sinful nor more worthy, 'we have a hope! Ever since by faith we looked to Jesus on the Cross, a hope full of glory has taken possession of our hearts! Is not this a marvelous thing?'[7]

The moment of resignation from reigning sin also remained vivid in Spurgeon's sense of true conversion. This, too, would form some analogy with converts. Spurgeon wrote to a perplexed soul that 'the hour is fresh in our memory when the divorce was signed between ourselves and our lusts. We can rejoice that we have now dissolved our league with hell. But, oh, how much we owe to sovereign grace.'

---

6. SEE 7:14, 15: 'Election: Its Defences and Evidences."
7. SEE 9:145.

Until regeneration, 'we never knew what it was to have peace with God until we had ceased to parley with sin.' A time of sickness was involved in the final resolution, a condition that led Spurgeon to confess, 'Our great anxiety was not lest we should die, but lest living we should find our holy feelings clear gone, and our piety evaporated.' If the reader feared the same, Spurgeon advised, 'Let us help you through it.'[8]

Spurgeon wanted to help people get rid of false views of repentance. In addition to biblical definitions and examples in this effort, he looked at several factors in his own experience that prompted true repentance. After one of the first times he discovered that God had truly answered a prayer and condescended to his personal supplication, 'I tell you that I loathed sin. I could not bear to do anything to grieve a God who really listened to my cry.' At another time of an obvious deliverance from trouble, he felt: 'How could I ever have been what I have been? How could I have lived as I have lived?' As he discovered that God's kindness always rose to meet his steps and would preserve him for ever as a beloved child, 'then did I hate sin more than I had ever done before.' He was grieved at any remaining bondage to sin and 'longed to be clean rid of every trace of sin!' In these events, it was not for fear of hell that he so advanced in turning from sin, but 'it was quite the reverse, but I hated sin because of God's love to me.' The lesson from his personal experience is that this 'is the way in which God brings repentance into the hearts of His children. He loves them so much and does so much for them, that they cannot continue any longer in sin.'[9]

Though Spurgeon believed thoroughly in God's sovereign timing in the application of efficacious grace for salvation, he also knew that sinners were no less responsible for their refusal to believe. He discussed, therefore, both the irrationality and the sinful pride of delaying coming to Christ. He illustrated the reality through

---

8. *The Saint and His Saviour*, pp. 75, 76, 81.
9. SEE 13:91.

his own experience describing explicitly an attitude once held by himself. 'Ah but surely,' saith one, 'I knew a person who was months and years in distress about his sin.' Spurgeon responded, 'I know such a person now.' This person was an 'unbelieving seeker' for five years but 'was a fool for being so. There was no reason why he should have been in the dark so long.' Though the issue of sin and salvation was in the light, 'his eyes were blindfolded by his own folly.' He could have believed in Jesus Christ and 'had the forgiveness of sin at once'.[10] One's struggle to salvation is not a fight against divine sovereignty, but against personal unbelief, pride, lust, and self-sufficiency. If true of himself, it was true of others.

In light of his strong belief in and contention for the doctrines of grace, Spurgeon looked at his experience as a type of how many might experience the effectual call of God. Using the experience of the boy Samuel as a model, Spurgeon said, 'I believe God was at work with my heart for years before I knew anything about Him.' Many relations, thoughts, and struggles of his childhood he thought were his own but knew not that it was the Lord's work. 'I knew I prayed and cried and groaned for mercy, but I did not know that was the Lord's work! I half thought it was my own. I did not know till afterwards, when I was led to know Christ as all my salvation and all my desire, that the Lord had called the child, for this could not have been the result of nature.' To those therefore, 'who are the beginners in the divine life, as long as your call is real, rest assured it is divine!' Given the marks of effectual calling – repentance, faith, desire for holiness, knowledge of truth, godliness, brotherliness, and love – one may be assured of his calling. 'By your character you may read your name!' He need not find it in the annals of eternity, for he can find it in his own affections. 'Though you cannot see God's hand in it, yet, by God's grace it is there!' In this way Spurgeon affirmed his calling, and so should they.[11]

---

10. SEE 7:355.
11. NPSP 5:241, 'Predestination and Calling.'

In speaking of the degree to which one must feel the horror of sin and the depth of remorse for it, Spurgeon warned, 'Beware of doting after this fashion. There must be sorrow for sin in every true believer, and there will be; but the best form of sorrow for sin generally follows forgiveness, and does not precede it.' How does he draw such a conclusion? Certainly Romans 7:13-24 would help, but the personal struggle seemed to give pastoral authenticity to his consolation. 'I never hated sin so much as when I knew that God had forgiven me. With all my soul do I sometimes sing to myself the choice lines of Mr Monsell:

> "My sins, my sins, my Saviour!
> How sad on thee they fall,
> Seen through thy gentle patience,
> I tenfold feel them all.
>
> I know they are forgiven,
> But still their pain to me
> Is all the grief and anguish
> They laid, my Lord, on Thee".[12]

The Chief of Sinners

Again, Spurgeon universalized Christ's ability to save by analyzing how powerful an act of grace it required to convert him. His own experience gave him hope for all others. 'For my part,' he remarked, 'I never can or will despair of the salvation of one of my fellow creatures now that I am myself saved.' He saw certain traits in his character and dispositional tendencies which made his conversion 'more remarkable than that of the conversion of anybody else'. He fostered, therefore, a hope 'concerning the most blasphemous, the most obstinate, the most unbelieving.' In the days of His flesh, Jesus opened the eyes of one born blind, which thing had never been known before. Most assuredly, then, He can come and deal with the very chief of sinners – ay, with sinners that are dead in sin

12. SEE 7:354.

– with sinners that lie rotting in their lusts, and He can make them to be saints!' He reasoned from his conversion to that of others and concluded, 'This is a fair argument: I am sure it is.'[13]

He illustrated the sovereignty of grace, the necessity of unconditional election, through recall of his personal sense of worthlessness and absolute emptiness of any merit at the point of his conversion: 'He saves because He will save. And if you ask me why He saves me, I can only say because He would do it.' Nothing he had could recommend him to God. He was the worst. 'When God saved me, I was the most abject, lost and ruined of the race. I lay before Him as an infant in my blood.' He assured the auditors of his pure powerlessness and unmitigated wretchedness. Note the intensity of the juxtaposition of his sin in relation to that of others. 'If you had something to recommend you to God, I never had. I will be content to be saved by grace, unalloyed, pure grace. I can boast of no merits. If you can do so, still I cannot. I must sing –

> "Free grace alone
> from the first to the last
> has won my affection
> and held my soul fast".'[14]

In 1891, preaching on 'God's Glorious and Everlasting Name', Spurgeon remarked: 'I am not sure, but I think that if God were to save any of you, I should not wonder at it so much as I often wonder that He should have saved me!' He still in this last year of ministry spoke to harlots, vagabonds, drunks, self-congratulatory religionists, and skeptics. None of these were beyond the reach of God, in Spurgeon's deepest perception. He testified, 'I sometimes ask myself whether I was converted because I was so headstrong and obstinate, that God might show how He can overcome obstinacy and how self-will can be made to sit at His feet.' Spurgeon saw himself as the chief of sinners, and would, therefore, lose hope for none.

---

13. *The Gospel for the People*, pp. 370-71.
14. NPSP 1:41.

A Guide to the Christian Life

Spurgeon saw himself as an example of the joy of beginning to work for Christ early in one's life. He commended this to others. In his book for new converts, *A Good Start: a Book for Young Men and Women*, he points to his own experience as a recommendation of life in Christ. 'Young men, I have tried the faith of Jesus Christ, and I have found it give me "pluck" – that is an old Saxon word, but it is exactly what I mean. It puts soul into a man, firmness, resolution, courage.'[15]

Throughout this book, Spurgeon used biblical examples to give exhortations to young believers, or on occasion to young unbelievers to spur them on to faith in Christ. In virtually every chapter, he gives some of his exhortations in light of his own experience of discipleship. Urging his readers to use every period of their life for the service of the Lord, Spurgeon noted: 'There is no time for work like the first hours of the day; and there is no time for serving the Lord like the very earliest days of youth.' He recalled his joy in early service. Though engaged in school all the week, Saturday afternoon 'was given to a tract-district, and to visiting the very poor within my reach.' Then on Sunday, he taught a class of children, and then a class of other Sunday School teachers. He believed that he spoke better then than in later years, 'for I spoke so tremblingly, but my heart went with it all.' Gradually he expanded and went to villages on Sunday to preach and eventually every night in the week. He spoke from the heart, for his only sources were 'the Word of God and my own experience'. He spoke, moreover, from his soul, probably mixed with 'much blundering and much weakness, and much youthful folly.' The desire, however, was intense and he would have laid down his life to bring someone to the feet of the Saviour.[16]

At the close of this book, Spurgeon reminisced about a recent trip he took to Stambourne where he saw a family that lived in the manse

---

15. *A Good Start*, p. 24.
16. Ibid, pp. 144, 145.

formerly occupied by his grandfather. He called that family around him, including children and grandchildren, and prayed for them, as Richard Knill had prayed for him decades before. 'Do you not see,' he asked, 'how that memory begat the prayer?' If he had been so affected by a prayer in that place, perhaps the prayer and the admonition would find wings of grace in the lives of those also. He wanted them 'to remember when they grew up my testimony of God's goodness to me'. Likewise, he presently shared his life's blessings 'for that same reason'. 'God has blessed me all my life long, and redeemed me from all evil, and I pray that He may be your God!'[17]

Spurgeon found in the talk of Jesus to the disciples on the road to Emmaus an opportunity to enforce these close analogies of spiritual life. Preaching from Luke 24 in 1887, Spurgeon pointed to the slowness of the disciples to believe the Scriptures and their folly in such hesitation. He admitted that in the midst of a commonly shared superabundance of evidence of divine faithfulness, disbelief was 'unreasonable and foolish'. Emphasizing the commonality of this experience, he continued: 'At least, I stand here to confess, that whenever I doubt my God it is on my part a superfluity of naughtiness. … If we disbelieve, is it not folly? If the Saviour does not call us fools, we are forced to call ourselves so.' He continued this identity of himself, his hearers, and the doubting disciples in making Jesus' charge common to all, spanning the centuries 'since I fear it applies to us as much as to them. Our hearts are full often sluggish in believing; at least, mine is so, and I suppose we are much alike.'[18]

Traits of Christian Ministry

Spurgeon's need for rest, like other elements of his humanity and his life of grace, was more prominent than that of others. He could give, therefore, strong encouragement to ministers of the gospel for times of renewal. 'You must get out of the world's din if you would renew

---

17. Ibid, p. 329.
18. SS 18:311, 314.

your cheerfulness.' He invited his men to the 'empty seat set for you in my engraving by the side of a rill, which ripples among the stones in the midst of a grove.' That is the kind of place Spurgeon found to be his hospital, oratory, armoury, observatory, and earthly heaven. Far better than 'medicine, stimulant, cordial, or lecturing,' Spurgeon commended 'quiet hours in calm retreats to God's hardworking servants in order to help their spirits up to the mark.' As with Paul in Arabia and Moses in the desert, the Spirit frequently blesses 'retirement to the restoration of the believer's joy and strength'.[19]

He saw in himself, even in 1856 on the sixth anniversary of his conversion, the necessity of God's giving a lesson in humility to ministers of the gospel. He recognized that he had been given immense favor from God in his ministry and had, because of it, the necessity of special works of humiliation. Suppose one is 'called to the great work of preaching the gospel. He is successful; God helps him – thousands wait at his feet, and multitudes hang upon his lips.' Such a man 'will have a tendency to be exalted above measure!' Suppose he looks to himself and too little to God. Those who know this will say, 'It is true.' When we begin to take glory for ourselves, a review of the lives of eminent saints will show that God 'made them feel that He was God, and beside Him there was none else.' Paul's thorn in the flesh was good for grace. At times, God will give a man 'such an insight into his own wicked and abominable heart that he will feel, as he comes up the pulpit stairs, that he does not deserve so much as to sit in his pew, much less to preach to his fellows!' Yes, even Spurgeon knew 'what it is to totter on the pulpit steps under a sense that the chief of sinners should scarcely be allowed to preach to others!' He did not believe, therefore, any could be a successful minister 'who is not taken into the depths and blackness of his own soul', to see that he is the least of all saints, who preaches not himself, but the unsearchable riches of Christ.[20]

---

19. S&T, 1866:105.
20. SS 1:11; NPSP 2:60. 'Sovereignty and Salvation.'

Every Christian minister must learn to deal with sorrow. Spurgeon had more than his share and he had found sufficient remedies. Knowing that his college students and former students would need help on this front, he preached in April 1891 a sermon entitled 'Honey in the Mouth' to his Pastors' College Evangelical Association. Not surprisingly, the answer was to see the glory of Christ and to see Him glorified. 'If the Holy Spirit glorifies Christ, that is the cure for every kind of sorrow. He is the Comforter.' He repeated the story of the tragedy at Surrey Gardens and the terrible depression that followed. Even the sight of a Bible made him cry. He stayed alone in the garden and 'was heavy and sad, for people had been killed and there I was, half dead, myself.' He remembered how he got back his comfort and was enabled again to preach. As he walked through the garden the words came, 'Him has God exalted with His right hand to be a Prince and a Savior.' They were only common soldiers, and should they die in the cause of his King, it would be well. Then the moment of commending his conclusion to his men: 'And so, I am sure, it is with every one of you, my Brothers, in this holy war! If our Lord and King is exalted, then let other things go which way they like.' We are 'perfectly willing to be forgotten, derided, slandered, or anything else that men please. The cause is safe, and the King is on the Throne.'

The Bible Tested and Proven

Very early in his Christian life Spurgeon had a brief bout with philosophical skepticism in relation to the Bible. He preached a sermon on the Bible during his first year at New Park Street. For any present who might be sceptics or free-thinkers, he did not profess any argument as a controversialist, but only showed that he too had such an intellectual dalliance. He set forth his own engagement with infidelity as a sufficient warning for all and as an answer to every claim that an opponent of biblical truth might make.

He stood only as a preacher 'of things that I know and feel'. He had an evil hour 'when once I slipped the anchor of my faith' and no longer 'moored myself hard by the coasts of Revelation'. He allowed personal reason influenced by free thought to carry him along at a rapid pace. He described the experience in brilliant and energetic visual images of light, pleasure at the sense of unbounded freedom, but then grinning fiends, rushing waves, and a doubt of his own existence. He passed by all the old 'landmarks of my faith'. He descended 'to the very verge of the dreary realms of unbelief,' even to the 'very bottom of the sea of infidelity'. 'The very extravagance of the doubt, proved its absurdity,' and a voice came to him, 'And can this doubt be true?' Startled by the absurdity of doubting his own existence, he awoke from the destructive mental journey, gradually he ascended and came again to the coasts of revelation. 'When I arose,' he testified, 'faith took the helm; from that moment, I doubted not.'[21]

Spurgeon had perfect mental persuasion from an abundance of evidences, both empirical and rational, that the Bible was indeed what it claimed to be – the Word of God. A deeper proof, however, was the fullness of his experience of its power both in his personal transformation and in its power to bring sinners to God, to love and praise and serve Him. He found his own experience in commending the power and truthfulness of Scripture a sufficient, a superabundant persuasive, for himself and others, of its divine origin. He certainly was not closed to compelling, irreducibly demonstrable evidence to the contrary, but that such could exist Spurgeon held out no chance of verification. 'I am open to conviction,' he maintained, 'but I shall never see the man that can convince me out of my experience, my conviction, my consciousness, my hope, my all.'[22] Every aspect of his personal religion and his experience in ministry amounted to a smothering torrent of empirical verification impossible to push aside. His thirst has been assuaged too many times for him to accept any argument that the water of life did not satisfy.

---

21. SS 1:29; NPSP 1:15.
22. SS 19:53.

Speaking of Scripture in all its parts and for its every purpose, Spurgeon asserted: 'The adaption of all this provision for our warfare we have already tested: the weapons of our armory are the very best; for we have made trial of them, and have found them so.' To others, therefore, he testified: 'Some of you, younger brethren, have only tested the Scripture a little as yet; but others of us, who are now getting grey, can assure you that we have tried the Word, as silver is tried in a furnace of earth; and it has stood every test.' Having lived for many years, without a single hour free of conflict, 'perpetually putting to the proof the Word of God,' he wanted to give the younger warriors his full assurance that 'it is equal to every emergency'. The sword has been laid with force to 'coats of mail and bucklers of brass' without suffering so much as a notch in its blade's edge. Neither broken nor blunted, 'It would cleave the devil himself, from the crown of his head to the sole of his foot' and suffer no sign of failure. Even as in the hands of Jesus, it is the Word of God for ministers today, and 'strengthens us when we remember the many conquests of souls which we have achieved through the sword of the Spirit!'[23]

Spurgeon asked if any had known conversions based on doctrines other than those in the Word of God. Could modern theology provide a testimony book of such conversions? Can one imagine conversions through preaching universal restoration, or doubtful inspiration, or the example view of the cross without its substitutionary sacrifice? 'Conversions by a gospel out of which all the gospel has been drained!' He challenged Bible-disbelievers to 'report changes of heart so wrought, and give us an opportunity of testing them.' Only then, under such a test, would he consider 'whether it is worth our while to leave that Word which we have tried in hundreds, and, some of us here, in many thousands of cases, and have always found effectual for salvation.' But such could never be the case. Such a contradictory wonder will never begin,

---

23. *The Greatest Fight in the World*, pp. 13, 14.

for the new birth is like a sour grape to such Bible critics. 'As we believe in the new birth, and expect to see it in thousands of cases,' Spurgeon testified, 'we shall adhere to that Word of truth by which the Holy Spirit works regeneration.' He intended to wage warfare by the 'old weapon of the sword of the Spirit, until we can find a better.' In all of his efforts to counsel and bring hope from despair, nothing could accomplish the impossible task but the Word of God. Recommending his own experience to his young students, Spurgeon affirmed: 'We know what we say, for we have witnessed the blessed facts: the Scriptures of truth, applied by the Holy Spirit, have brought peace and joy to those who sat in darkness and in the valley of the shadow of death.'[24]

Spurgeon viewed his experiential certainty of the Bible's inspiration and power in the image of a wick that had soaked up the oil into it. 'The gospel,' he reflected, 'is something more than a matter of faith; it has so mingled with my being as to be a part of me.' Faith in the orthodox creed no longer is a matter of choice but essential to his very being. When invited to examine the present arguments, he declined, for he could smell that they were wrong. They began by denying too much that was essential for life and eternity, and so could never perform the healings he had seen. 'Bind philosophy around an aching heart, and see if it will relieve the agony. Take a draught of modern thought, and see if it will cure despair. Go to death-beds, where men are looking into eternity, and see if the principles of the skeptical school can help the sick to die in triumph.'[25] He had for too long seen the effects of Scripture true to its claims to lay it aside for a new and untested, and thus unproven, way of life.

Spurgeon believed that the long experience of forty years and printing sermons for thirty-six years had entitled him 'to speak about the fullness and richness of the Bible, as a preacher's book.'

---

24. Ibid., pp. 14, 15.
25. *An All Round Ministry*, pp. 125-26.

Its inexhaustibility gave it endless variety and freshness, and he had touched only the hem of its garment. Preaching would continue in eternity, for the principalities and powers would learn even more to marvel at the gospel when spoken from the fully sanctified lips of gospel preachers – a parish of millions of leagues surrounded by innumerable pure intelligences. We will be marvels of grace verifying the wisdom of the mystery of God manifest in the flesh. Each of us will have his own tale to tell of our experience of infinite love. 'If such be the case, our Bibles will suffice for ages to come for new themes every morning, and for fresh songs and discourses world without end.'[26]

---

26. *The Greatest Fight in the World,* p. 18.

8

'AN EARNEST CONTENTION
FOR THE FAITH'

• • • • • • • • • • • • • • • • • • • •

In speaking to his ministerial students about the 'Minister in these Times', Spurgeon said, 'I have received a measure of pity because I am in opposition to so many.' He advised that they should save their pity for him and give it to the other side. When a friend warned Spurgeon that the baptismal regeneration controversy had put him in hot water, he responded that his water was not hot but rather cool. Instead he stoked the flames for those who should feel the water to be hot, and he was doing his best to make the water 'so hot that they will be glad to get out of it'. He did not wish to fight; but when he did, he hoped 'that the pity will be needed by those with whom we contend.'[1]

Spurgeon's Early and Unabated Awareness of the Need for Controversy

Spurgeon tasted resistance to truth early in his Christian life when efforts in teaching the doctrines of grace had resulted in some sparks of dissension. In June 1850 he remarked that the 'majority of Newmarket Christians' were 'rather Arminian'. In the same letter he told his mother, 'My enemies are many, and they hate me with cruel

---

1. *An All Round Ministry*, p. 395.

hatred.' In spite of it, Jehovah Jesus was at his side.[2] In November of 1850 he wrote his aunt and uncle: 'Let the whole earth and even God's professing people, cast out my name as evil; my Lord and Master, He will not. I glory in the distinguishing grace of God, and will not, by the grace God, step one inch from my principles, or think of adhering to the present fashionable sort of religion.'[3]

In 1856, Spurgeon preached on 'Gospel Missions' before a missionary society. He pointed to minimalist doctrinal conviction as undermining 'successful prosecution of the gospel'. As he compared the needs of their present time to the needs and solutions of different historical eras of the Church, Spurgeon proclaimed: 'But we will enter our earnest hearty protest against the coldness and the lethargy of the times – and as long as this, our tongue, shall move in our mouth – we will protest against the laxity and false Doctrine so rampant throughout the Churches.' He looked for a reformation both 'in Doctrine and Spirit'.

In 1871, writing an analysis of 'Advanced Thought', Spurgeon observed the irony of such advancement. Men of liberal thought and high culture would characterize the Christian as shackled in 'bonds of dogmatism and the slavery of creed'. Spurgeon spared no scorn for these self-appointed governors of true enlightenment; He saw through them and argued that 'they are not liberal, but intolerant to the last degree.' Their disdain for 'those poor simpletons who abide by the old faith' could not be hidden. They are neither enlightened nor advanced while indulging in 'old, worn-out heresies'.[4]

In 1875, Spurgeon preached on 'Jesus, the Stumbling Stone of Unbelievers.' While sparing neither the Jews, the Roman Emperors, the Arians, nor the corrupt house of Roman Catholicism as enemies of the Cornerstone, as sole mediator, Spurgeon saved his most potent warning for enlightened prophets of nineteenth-century criticism.

---

2. Murray, *Letters*, p. 28.

3. Charles Spurgeon, *The Letters of C. H. Spurgeon* (1923). Accessed 29 March 2020: http://www.romans45.org/spurgeon/misc/letters.htm.

4. S&T, 1871 (November).

Though in a different cloak, he saw the same assassin lurking in the darkness. He saw 'another opposition which will be as difficult to cope with as any that has gone before'. Mustering within the Church of God were men 'who say they hate all creeds, meaning that they despise all Truth.' They love their positions as ministers, 'yet tread under foot all that we hold sacred.' They go slowly, measuring out the rate of heresy and infidelity little by little, gradually gathering courage fully to vent their unbelief. 'Credophobia is maddening many,' Spurgeon warned. 'They appear to fear lest they should believe anything,' and want to make room for all religions 'except the only true one!' Spurgeon made his protest clear and strong, but consented that 'if it should be lost amidst the general popular clamor, and if the nations should be drunk again with the wine of this fornication, and turn aside to error, what matters it to the ultimate success of the eternal Cause?' He was sure that Christ would reign as king, and the covenant 'sealed with blood shall be sure to all the chosen seed!' Despite all that can be done against God's truth by men or devils, 'not one Elect soul shall be lost, not one soul redeemed by blood shall be snatched out of the Redeemer's hand!' Likewise, 'His people's earnest contention for the faith shall honor Him; their patient suffering shall give Him praise.'[5]

Some close observers of Spurgeon's life and gifts have lamented that he gave himself so much to controversy. They have argued that he was not apt for it and that it robbed time and energy from his more fitting work of evangelism and benevolence. Spurgeon would not agree. He considered it vital to his call as a guardian of truth. Also, he was well aware of the tools needed for effective controversy. These can be summarized in the classic categories of rhetoric.

The three classic elements of rhetoric are logos, pathos, and ethos. Logos involves presentation of the arguments employing facts, logic, evidence, synthesizing of data, and careful arrangement of ideas to give the greatest climax to the argument. Pathos exhibits

---

5. MTP 21:1224: 'Jesus, the Stumbling Stone of Unbelievers.'

the emotional depth of one's convictions. Earnest emotion, inflexible conviction, and deep-seated persuasion give riveting intensity to logos. Pathos shows that the controversialist really believes his point and feels the weight and importance of it. Pathos employs the emotions in order to reach the emotions or affections of the audience. Pathos demonstrates that elevated and pure feelings join with the argument in the effort to demonstrate the urgency and relevance of the point. Jonathan Edwards famously wrote in *Some Thoughts Concerning the Revival*, 'Our people need not so much to have their heads stored as the hearts moved.' Ethos concerns the atmosphere that surrounds the speaker himself. Is he a credible person; had he gained a reputation for transparent, truthful character? Spurgeon's personal courage and his obvious transcendent love of truth above popularity or approval impregnated his ethos with powerful credibility.

Spurgeon had mastered the rhetoricians' types of arguments, figures of speech, dialectical method, and other matters of public discourse. He was not weak on *logos* or hesitant to use closely-tuned logic and a variety of persuasive techniques.

Nevertheless, Spurgeon focused mainly on *pathos* and *ethos*. This was not accidental but was an intentional engagement of persuasive method on his part. Preaching early in his time in London, Spurgeon said, 'Now, there are some gentlemen present who are saying, "Now we shall see whether Mr Spurgeon has any logic in him." No, you won't sirs,' Spurgeon hypothesized his response, 'because I never pretend to exercise it. I hope I have the logic which can appeal to men's hearts; but I am not very prone to use the less powerful logic of the head, when I can win the heart in another manner.' Pathos gained ascendency over logos. 'But if it were needful,' he continued, 'I should not be afraid to prove that I know more of logic, and of many other things, than the little men who undertake to censure me.' Confident that he was fully armed in all requisite aspects of persuasive argument, he continued: 'It were well if they knew how to hold their tongues, which is at least a fine part of rhetoric. My argument shall be such as, I trust, will appeal to the heart and conscience, although it may not exactly please those who are always so fond of syllogistic demonstration.'[6] Spurgeon had decided to go for pathos and ethos – heart and conscience. To persuade the head without gaining the affections and the life would be no Christianity at all.

Spurgeon did not fall into controversy by mistake or even with reluctance. He had a purpose in naming his monthly magazine *The Sword and the Trowel*. He intended to keep both instruments busy in their respective fields. 'Foes have felt the sword far more than they would care to confess,' he noted, while 'friends have seen the work of the trowel on the walls of Zion to their joy and rejoicing'. Confessing his readiness to be a defender of the faith, he told the Baptist Missionary Society: 'When the gage of battle is thrown down, I am not the man to refuse to take it up.'

Three Types of Controversies

Spurgeon's controversies fall into three major types. Controversy at the first level came at the point of immediate conflict over specific scriptural teaching on particular issues that did not threaten orthodoxy. This involved a clash of messages and a clash of confessions. Spurgeon had much to say in this area and spread his remarks over a wide field including persons, denominations, and movements. Worship practice, preaching style, evangelism practice, and the ordinances or sacraments were some of the issues he confronted occasionally.

A second type of controversy focused on the theological differences that he had with other publications, including periodicals and books. For the most part this type involved a single interaction but on occasions resulted in prolonged, and sometimes bitter, insulting exchanges. The constant harangue of *The Christian World* sometimes led Spurgeon to what he felt were necessary responses.

---

6. SS 1:371-72.

Books on theological or ecclesiological issues from Joseph Parker to J. C. Ryle often elicited a spurgeonic interaction.

The third level of conflict emerged with those that held a confessional position ostensibly, but felt themselves justified in functioning in opposition to it. Sometimes their theology was better than the confession, but the privilege of position influenced their adherence to the statement. Spurgeon admonished them to leave their church and place themselves at the behest of divine provision. Others ministered outside the parameters of, or in opposition to, their confessions. They professed orthodoxy but functioned in heterodoxy. They believed less and worse that the confession proclaimed. For these, Spurgeon felt special alarm; he was disdainful of their hypocrisy. If a minister is found to be inconsistent with the standards, what should be done? Spurgeon had a succinct and reasonable approach to the problem.

> They should have a patient hearing that they may have opportunity to explain, and if it be possible to their consciences, may sincerely conform; but if the divergence be proven, they must with all the courtesy consistent with decision be made to know that their resignation is expected, or their expulsion must follow. The church which does not do this has only one course before it is consistent with righteousness; if it be convinced that the standards are in error and the preacher right, it ought at all hazards to amend its standards, and if necessary to erase every letter of its creed, so as to form itself on a model consistent with the public teaching which it elects, or with the latitude which it prefers. However much of evil might come of it, such a course would be unimpeachably consistent, so consistent indeed that we fear few ordinary mortals will be able to pursue it; but the alternative of maintaining a hollow compact, based on a lie, is as degrading to manliness as to Christianity.[7]

As Spurgeon worked through the many controversies that punctuated his ministry, he developed a sense of how they should be conducted. In writing to one of the figures involved in the Downgrade controversy,

---

7. S&T, November 1871:73.

Spurgeon requested: 'Let us daily pray for each other, in reference to the work which lies before us, that we may be faithful unto death – faithful not only to the doctrines of truth, but to the spirit of love – warring our warfare without trace of personal bitterness, but with stern resolve to spare none of the errors which insult the sacrifice of our Lord, destroy the way of salvation in this life, and then seek to delude men with the dream of salvation after death.'[8]

Specific Controversies – Minor Skirmishes

Rivulet Controversy

The 'Rivulet Controversy' was one of the first to which Spurgeon contributed. A book of poetry written by Thomas T. Lynch brought about amazingly broad and energized response from religious papers. Supposedly proposed by Lynch as a hymnal for Christian worship, the texts, in the opinion of many, were little more than expressions of deism and just the sort of thing that a Unitarian might employ. Spurgeon joined the opposition in a piece entitled 'Mine Opinion'. 'If I should ever be on amicable terms with the chief of the Ojibewas,' Spurgeon mused, 'I might suggest several verses from Mr Lynch as a portion of a liturgy to be used on the next occasion when he bows before the Great Spirit of the West Wind.' Spurgeon called on the Delawares, Mohawks, Choctaws, Chickasaws, Blackfeet, Pawnees, Shawnees, and Cherokees (showing an impressive display of knowledge of native Americans, with whom he had sincere sympathy) to find in Lynch's collection their 'primitive faith most sweetly rehearsed'.[9] Like others he found no way to recommend its contents for Christian worship.

Joseph Parker

When Joseph Parker, the brilliant pastor at the City Temple, arrived in London, Spurgeon welcomed him. He would give a more profound and learned *gravitas* to the cause of dissent in London. Soon, however,

---

8. Pike, 6:291.
9. *Autobiography*, 1:478

Spurgeon developed reservations about Parker's imprecise theological convictions. He admired his writing style and his originality but wanted him to be more definite in his commitment to evangelical theology. After years of alternating friendly praise and reserved criticism, Parker took advantage of the Downgrade controversy to register snide remarks about Spurgeon's Calvinistic commitments. 'When people ask me what I think of Spurgeon, I always ask which Spurgeon.' Did the questioner refer to the Tabernacle or the orphanage – to Spurgeon's head or his heart? While Parker saw the orphanage as all beauty and love, he simply hated the Calvinism of the Tabernacle. He held it in reproach as he would 'selfishness and blasphemy'. He characterized it as 'leering, slavering, sly-winking' arrogance that says, 'Bless the Lord we are all right, booked straight through to heaven first-class.'[10]

Spurgeon did not hesitate to call out Parker on his insistent theological moderatism. Parker's restatement of *The Priesthood of Christ* had nothing in it that Spurgeon could make himself commend. He hoped that some in Parker's own denomination would have enough courage to expose the 'mischievous tendencies of this book'. To the chapter on 'Ultimate Aspects of Christ's Priesthood', Spurgeon gave the ultimate denunciation in calling it 'the most evil piece of writing it was ever our misery to read'. Parker wrote in such a way as to avoid being blamed specifically for positions explored in the book, all of which Spurgeon pronounced as 'unutterably bad'. Even an honest infidel should dislike Parker's slipperiness and lack of resolve to shoulder the burden of his doctrinal proposals. 'The underlying idea of preaching one thing when you mean another, disguise it how you please, and justify it how you may,' Spurgeon fired, 'is simply detestable.'[11]

Pretensions of Science
Spurgeon had deep appreciation for the advancements in health, communications, comfort, technology, and human flourishing

---

10. Murray, *Forgotten Spurgeon,* p. 181.
11. S&T, January 1877, p. 42.

produced by true science. He kept abreast of developments in medicine, the incipiency of photography, electric lights, and the phonograph. He considered science the friend of divine revelation. 'For our own part,' he affirmed, 'we hail the light that streams upward from the dark places of the earth.' He welcomed archaeology, geology, and physical geography as 'the very sciences that God has ordained to be His witnesses, to frustrate the tokens of liars, to make diviners mad, and to confirm the word of His servants the prophets.'[12] 'We have no fear,' he commented, 'for the result of the conflict between science and religion: the God of Nature is the God of the Bible, and when we read both aright we shall not see conflict, but deep unity and harmony.'

When scientists sought to use their status, however, to pose as metaphysicians, Spurgeon called their bluff. He found himself utterly opposed to the flood of evolutionary literature following the publication of Darwin's *The Origin of Species.* The theory in Spurgeon's view was atheistic and illogical. In a review of *Darwinism and Design; or, Creation by Evolution,* Spurgeon contended that to argue for design from Darwinism was irrational. He found completely unacceptable the idea that evolution assumed 'we have a chain of effects producing causes more powerful than themselves'. Darwinism and design are mutually exclusive. The move from inorganic to organic, vegetative to instinctual, instinctual to rational has never been observed nor can this assumed transition be duplicated. After reading *Explorations and Adventures in Equatorial Africa,* in a clever, but much-maligned and ridiculed lecture, Spurgeon spoke to an image of a gorilla's head, 'I believe there is a great gulf fixed between us, so that they who would pass from us to you cannot; neither can they to us who would pass from thence.' Papers drew caricatures of a professorial gorilla lecturing Spurgeon and examining his head. Spurgeon called scientific infidelity a 'hard task master that put far more burdens on the mind than biblical orthodoxy ever did'.

---

12. S&T, June 1881, p. 286.

In an unusual interaction with geological science, Spurgeon prepared himself for the possible acceptance of their growing assertion about the earth's age as being far beyond, millions of years beyond, the apparent witness of Scripture to its age as less than ten-thousand years. Noting layers of death in strata prior to the time of the appearance of humans – according to the geological theories – Spurgeon hypothesized that 'those deaths before Adam [were] the antecedent consequences of a sin which was then uncommitted.' He justified this by establishing an analogous relation between salvation before propitiation and death before the commission of sin. 'If by the merits of Jesus there was salvation before He had offered His atoning sacrifice, I do not find it hard to conceive that the foreseen demerits of sin may have cast the shadow of death over the ages which preceded man's transgressions.'[13]

The Cigar Controversy

The memorable defense of smoking given in the Tabernacle came on the occasion of George Pentecost's visit in September 1874. Asked to give some personal reflections on Spurgeon's call to holiness in his sermon, Pentecost told of his decision to relinquish his indulgence in 'the best cigar which could be bought'. After Pentecost explained what led him to that conviction and encouraged others to find a similar point of scrupulosity for the sake of holiness, Spurgeon rose with the task of saving himself, his guest, and making clear the point of his sermon. 'Well, dear friends,' he began, according to the *Christian World* report, 'you know that some men can do to the Glory of God what to other men would be a sin.' Notwithstanding Pentecost's personal conviction, Spurgeon declared, 'I intend to smoke a good cigar to the Glory of God, before I go to bed tonight.' He saw no commandment in Scripture, 'Thou shalt not smoke,' and he had no intention of introducing the eleventh or the twelfth commandment. Some may have developed a conscience against it,

---

13. *Christ's Glorious Achievements*, pp. 106-07.

just as another may believe he should not get his boots blacked; if so, the one must not smoke and the other must refrain from boot-blackening, for whatever is not of faith is sin. The fact is, Spurgeon emphasized, 'I have been speaking to you about real sin, and not about listening to mere quibbles and scruples.' Spurgeon was not ashamed of his smoking and, therefore, 'I mean to smoke to the glory of God.'[14]

A firestorm arose around these impromptu remarks. Spurgeon responded with a longer defense in a letter to the editor of the *Daily Telegraph*. He regretted the occasion that prompted the 'unpremeditated remarks' as well as the tone of the article that reported it. Spurgeon observed the arising of a 'Pharisaic system which adds to the commands of God the precepts of men'. He did not intend for their sneers to interrupt either his liberty or his serenity. To the degree that the expression 'smoking to the glory of God' had an ill sound, Spurgeon did not justify it; but its intent was not abstract but specific and contextualized.

> When I have found intense pain relieved, a weary brain soothed and calm, refreshing sleep obtained by a cigar I have felt grateful to God, and have blessed His name; that is what I meant and by no means did I use sacred words triflingly. If through smoking, I had wasted an hour of my time – if I had stinted my gifts to the poor – if I had rendered my mind less vigorous – I trust I should see my fault and turn from it; but he who charges me with these things shall have no answer but my forgiveness.[15]

W. M. Hutchins responded with a lengthy investigation of Spurgeon's accusations of Pharisaism. Did Spurgeon not care about his universal influence, and that such a publicly embraced habit could only result in damage? Were the temperance organizations in his own Tabernacle pharisaical? Was Paul improperly persnickety and inventing new commandments when he refused to embrace his freedom of eating

---

14. Fulton, p. 345.
15. Ibid., p. 347.

meat should such eating harm his brother? Spurgeon's principle can be distilled to this – 'that a Christian man is at liberty to exercise self-indulgence in all matters against which there is not direct and express command in Scripture.'[16]

Spurgeon did not give up his cigars. William E. Hatcher, who recently had quit the habit as a Virginia Baptist pastor, joined Spurgeon in a smoke in 1888. He tells an amusing story about the event and at the time indicated his knowledge of the Pentecost incident and its history in the press.[17]

The Question of Slavery

In 1859 a fugitive slave, John Andrew Jackson, gave a testimony in a midweek service at New Park Street, taking an hour to describe his suffering, his escape, and his conversion. Greatly moved, and reflecting the mood of the entire congregation, Spurgeon called slavery, 'the foulest blot that ever stained a national escutcheon, and may have to be washed out with blood.' Though he considered America a glorious country in many ways, he believed that it might have to learn its lesson about slavery 'at the point of a bayonet' or have true freedom carved into her with a bowie knife or sent 'home to her heart with revolvers'. 'Better far should it come to this issue,' he advocated, 'that North and South should be rent asunder, and the States of the Union shivered into a thousand fragments, than that slavery should be suffered to continue.'[18] Spurgeon was more convinced of its evil and the necessity to correct it than he was of the evil of war.

When his references to slavery were omitted in the American printing of his sermons, Spurgeon learned of it and responded in heated terms in a letter to be published in an 'influential paper in America'. He wrote: 'I believe slavery to be a crime of crimes, a soul-destroying

---

16. Ibid., p. 353.
17. William E. Hatcher, *Along the Trail of the Friendly Years* (New York: Fleming H. Revell Company, 1910), pp. 242-49.
18. Carlile, p. 159.

sin, and an iniquity which cries for vengeance.' When asked to write an article on the Christian view of slavery, Spurgeon declined in light of pressing engagements and pressures involved in the building of the Metropolitan Tabernacle, but he did manage a substantial letter to the *Watchman and Reflector* in which he reiterated: 'I do from my inmost soul detest slavery anywhere and everywhere, and although I commune at the Lord's Table with men of all creeds, yet with a slave-holder I have no fellowship of any kind or sort.'

This plain speech about a deeply divisive topic brought severe consequences for Spurgeon's popularity and pocketbook in America. The sale of his sermons, which was massive, was virtually ended for the years 1860-65. He knew this would happen. Manstealing, however, inextricably identified with slavery, is listed by Paul (1 Tim. 1:10) as a particular violation of the ten commandments. The principle was so clear that no amount of political or pragmatic concerns could sway him in a different direction. His bound volumes of books were committed to the fire in public ceremonies in several places in the South.[19]

Major Eruptions of Controversy

The Baptismal Regeneration controversy

Spurgeon preached a sermon in 1864 on Baptismal Regeneration and the evangelicals in the Church of England. They pledged to uphold the *Book of Common Prayer* including its baptismal theology while not believing a doctrine to which they swore fealty. The Gorham case of 1849-51 [George Gorham, Evangelical Bishop of Exeter] ruled evangelicals could serve in the Church of England.

Referring to his efforts to find a point of fellowship with Anglicans, Spurgeon lamented: 'We have been cultivating friendship with those who are either unscriptural in creed or else dishonest, who either believe baptismal regeneration, or profess that they do, and swear before God that they do when they do not.' No more truce, no more parley between God's servants and time servers.

---

19. Carlile, pp. 159-61.

One evangelical responded: 'The doctrine of baptismal regeneration is decidedly a Popish error; but the Church of England does not hold it, nor do her good ministers preach it; and this is proved by nearly all the published replies made to Mr Spurgeon's sermon.' Another responded: 'I meet this statement with a simple denial; the evangelical clergy do not, in the sense described by Mr Spurgeon, *believe that the Church of England teaches baptismal regeneration,* and therefore do "not swear before God that they do when they do not;" and in this lies the whole fallacy of Mr Spurgeon's statements.' In addition, Baptist Noel who had left Anglicanism to become a Baptist and was highly respected in all quarters asked Spurgeon: 'Did you remember that your words were blasting, as far as they were received, the memory of some of the most excellent men who have ever lived?' Also, Noel wrote, Spurgeon had violated a principle of the Evangelical Alliance 'to avoid all rash and groundless insinuations, personal imputations, or irritating allusions.'[20]

Spurgeon's sermon was met with disdain by the High Church party of Anglicans. One of them published an article entitled 'The Evil-speaking and ignorance of Mr C. H. Spurgeon.' The Evangelicals felt betrayed by Spurgeon. Some responded by insulting his intelligence and proclaiming his inability to follow a cogent theological argument. One Anglican minister responded with regret that so much attention had been given to the railings of 'that young minister'. Rather, he 'is to be pitied, because his entire want of acquaintance with theological literature leaves him utterly unfit for the determination of such a question.' Barely concealing his condescension, the respondent remarked that this issue was not a question 'of mere doctrine, but of what may be called historical theology.' To engage Spurgeon 'would be to as little purpose as to attempt to hold a logically-constructed argument with a child unacquainted with logical terms.'[21]

---

20. Pike, 3:97, 99.
21. Pike, 3:104.

The opposition and ridicule left Spurgeon undaunted. He responded, not only through comments in the *Sword and the Trowel*, but by preaching 'Children brought to Christ and not to the Font' and another entitled 'Thus Saith the Lord, or the Book of Common Prayer Weighed in the Balances of the Sanctuary.'

Not cowed in the least by the strength of the opposition, still as late as 1868 Spurgeon found the doctrine of baptismal regeneration a diabolical deceit behind which consciences hid for both assurance (false!) and avoidance of real gospel faith. 'Were you christened?' he asked. 'Oh! The blessedness of that christening,' sarcasm oozing. Then with perfect and brutal frankness he called the doctrine 'a thing which is as gross a piece of superstition as ever was practiced by Mahomet, which has no more warrant in the word of God than the baptism of bells or the burning of Hindoo widows.' It is, instead, an 'idle farce' and a 'wicked mockery'. All this 'god-fathering and godmothering' is not God's ordinance but an 'invention of the Pope of Rome'. Pity those who receive it as 'a soul-saving thing' that 'regenerates the children that are subjected to it'. Such folly is followed by other apparent conveyors of grace that are equally rites of 'imbecility' that have 'no scriptural warrant'.[22]

The Downgrade Controversy

The most devastating controversy, and the one that perhaps shortened Spurgeon's life by its emotional aggravation to an already distressed and depressed frame, began in March of 1887 when Spurgeon published an article by Robert Shindler. The article and the controversy were called 'The Downgrade'. After identifying theological decline in various denominations, Shindler pointed to the loss of the commitment to inspiration and consequent infallibility of Scripture as the fatal step. What doctrine, dependent on revelation for its propagation, could possibly survive such a loss of foundational authority.

---

22. MTP 14:339, 340: 'The Wall Daubed with Untempered Mortar.'

Reaction against Shindler's articles led Spurgeon to engage the issue personally. In October 1887 he queried if the orthodox were to remain in union with those who hold Universalism or Purgatory and deny the inspiration of Scripture, the Fall, and the great sacrifice of Christ for sin. Some may have such liberty, but we must take caution 'that we do not become accomplices with those who teach another gospel' or 'have avowedly another God'.[23]

The next month Spurgeon again emphasized how faltering the new kind of thinking was in relation to the central gospel truth of divine revelation. At the time he was writing this article, he also wrote S. H. Booth, the Secretary of the Baptist Union, 'I must withdraw from that society.' He begged Booth not to send anyone to ask for reconsideration and said that his reasons for withdrawal 'are set forth in *The Sword and the Trowel* for November'. This is a part of his reasoning.

> We who believe Holy Scripture to be the inspired truth of God cannot have fellowship with those who deny the authority from which we derive all our teaching. We go to our pulpits to save a fallen race, and believe that they must be saved in this life, or perish for ever: how can we profess brotherhood with those who deny the fall of man, and hold out to him the hope of another probation after death? They have all the liberty in the world, and we would be the last to abridge it; but that liberty cannot demand our cooperation.[24]

Booth responded with a sense of distress and informed Spurgeon that he had wounded the hearts of many 'who honour and love you more than you have any idea of.' Spurgeon, having addressed the doctrinal issues on many occasions without calling any names of offenders, stated: 'It is a great grief to me that hitherto many of our most honoured friends in the Baptist Union have, with strong determination, closed their eyes to serious divergences from truth.'[25]

---

23. S&T, October 1887, p. 513. 'The Case Proved.'
24. S&T, November 1887, p. 559. 'A Fragment on the Downgrade Controversy.'
25. Pike, 6:291.

Members of the council claimed that Spurgeon had not 'brought any charge as to laxity of faith and practice such as would have justified them in laying it before the Council of the assembly.' In January 1888, the Council of the Union passed a resolution that the charges insinuated in Spurgeon's correspondence with members of the council and in his publications 'ought not to have been made'. This was viewed as a censure of Spurgeon by the man himself as well as by others. John Clifford objected to the perception and wrote: 'In short, the issue is this: that Mr Spurgeon may accuse the whole Union of anything he pleases, but no one among us may presume to whisper doubt about his action in a single case.'

Spurgeon himself wrote a response to this censure by the Union in February 1888. He exposed two fatal inconsistencies. First, he saw as spurious the stated intention to discuss that 'the unity of the denomination can be maintained in truth, and love, and good works.' Second, Spurgeon discussed the useless venture of seeking fellowship on the basis of partial agreement to a body of truth. 'How can we unite except upon some great common truths? Baptism by immersion is true, but it is meaningless without the most essential pillars of orthodoxy and the surety of divine revelation. To erect a pyramid on its apex would bring down the whole edifice.' He felt no fellowship with an immersed man 'if in other matters he is false to the teachings of Holy Scripture'.

The controversy demonstrated the need for a clearly stated creed. It is no hindrance to ministry, nor a block to fellowship, nor an usurpation of the authority of Scripture. Instead, it enhances all and gives clarity to one's intent. The slippery language of the confession set forth settled nothing but Spurgeon's distrust of the mixture of voices in the Union.

As he finished his response to the censure, he noted his continued opposition to doctrinal decline wherever it appeared. Though he had receded from any personal involvement in the Union's affairs in particular, 'so far as it takes its part in the common departure from the truth, it will have to put up with my strictures, although it has so graciously kicked me under pretext of deliberation.' He asked for prayer from those who joined him in the struggle for doctrinal fidelity.[26]

Modernism invaded even the College Conference. Spurgeon, when aware of opposition from within the ranks of his own graduates, dissolved the conference and reorganized it on the basis of a newly-minted confession designed for the time. None but those who would vote 'yes' to this arrangement would be included as members of the conference. Spurgeon was gladdened as responses began to come in the post. 'It is no small solace that nearly four hundred have voted yes right straight; and it will be a still greater joy, if, after the explanation given, many of you will do the like. By your love to me,' he continued, 'I beseech you do nothing which would be half-hearted. We can do each other more good apart in open-hearted honesty than together with suppressed ill-will.' His service in this conference had been a great joy and he hoped it would continue to be so, but he wanted no advocate of 'advanced thought' in the ranks. He would thank them to go their way and leave him as 'an immovable old man'. Why would any advocate of the modern doctrines and methods wish 'to stay with such an old fogey as I am'? They should leave him, perhaps as an object of pity, but surely not of enmity, for he had only sought to do all his men good according to his 'light and capacity'. He hoped for the blessings of God's grace on 'the faithful among you, leading you to be wholly and boldly on the Lord's side in this day when men cannot endure sound doctrine!'[27]

Even to the End

When his continued strictures seemed to fall on deaf ears, Spurgeon, nevertheless, did not diminish his calls for contending for the truth. Sometimes he felt that his sword landed on a 'sack of wool', so soft and undefined were the confessional lines of progressive thought.

---

26. S&T, February 1888, p. 83.
27. Pike, 6:298.

'But what if earnest protests accomplish nothing,' Spurgeon contemplated, 'because of the invincible resolve of the infatuated to abide in fellowship with the inventors of false doctrine?' His answer – 'Well, we shall at least have done our duty. We are not responsible for success. If the plague cannot be stayed, we can at least die in the attempt to remove it.' He looked with hope at every witness against 'Anythingarianism' as some hindrance to its complete dominance. 'It may be,' Spurgeon reflected, 'that in some one instance a true witness is strengthened by our word, or a waverer is kept from falling; and this is not mean reward.' He recognized that his testimony was contemptible to many and, in truth, may 'in itself be feeble enough to be open to ridicule'. He considered himself, however, one of the weak things of the world that, in time, would overcome the mighty.[28]

One year after his resignation from the Baptist Union, Spurgeon preached a message entitled 'No Compromise'. He compared Rebekah's separation from her homeland and her family to become the wife of Isaac. Suppose he had gone to Nahor's house to spare Rebekah the pain of parting from friends and from traveling. 'If those things could have kept her back, what would she have been worth to Isaac?' Nor can we go down to the world in order to gain acceptance. In the same way that Rebekah would have been a poor wife had she not been willing to separate and make a journey to reach her husband, so all converts the church may gain by 'softening down its doctrine, and by becoming worldly, will not be worth one bad farthing a gross. When we get them, the next question will be, "How can we get rid of them?"' In his stewardship to be clear of the blood of all men, Spurgeon had preached God's truth with no compromise foisted upon it by modern skepticism. He gave clear presentation of all its peculiarities, and, in order not to stultify his testimony, he had cut himself 'clear of those who err from the faith, and even from those who associate with them.'[29]

---

28. S&T, April 1888:159. 'Progressive Theology.'
29. SS 19:345-66.

Controversy was not among the most pleasant tasks of a God-called minister, but was, nevertheless, necessary for fighting the good fight. 'Every man who keeps aloof from the struggle for the sake of peace, will have the blood of souls upon his head,' Spurgeon insisted. These are no minor matters, no intra-mural rivalries between true brothers, but 'It is Bible or no Bible, Atonement or no Atonement, which we have now to settle.' No beclouding terms remain; the discussion has ripped back all the layers and the bottom has appeared: 'every lover of the Lord Jesus should feel himself called upon to take his part in an earnest contention for the faith once for all delivered to the saints.'[30]

---

30. S&T, December 1889:2. 'This Must be a Soldier's Battle.'

9

'GOD WAS SLANDERED
IN PARADISE'

• • • • • • • • • • • • • • • •

From Newmarket in February 1850, Spurgeon wrote to his mother about his desires to be useful in the work of the gospel. While he longed to do something, he also longed to maintain 'a sense of my own weakness, nothingness, and utter inability to do anything in and of myself, – I pray God that I may never lose it.' He had no doubt that should he be cut off from the constant supply of strength from God, 'I shall be taken by the Philistines in my own wicked heart, and have mine eyes for ever closed to all spiritual good.'[1]

In July, Spurgeon reported an increased amount of gospel labor while still expressing an absolute dependence on God and distrust of himself. 'I trust the Lord is weaning me daily from all self-dependence, and teaching me to look at myself as less than nothing.' Without a constant supply of grace, he would be 'perfectly dead'. This conviction, however, no longer depended on mere self-examination, but found reinforcement from rising opposition from others. 'My enemies are many, and they hate me with cruel hatred,' he wrote; 'yet with Jehovah Jesus on my side, why should I fear? I will march on in His almighty strength to certain conquest and

---

1. Murray, *Letters.* To his mother on 19 February 1850.

victory.' Spurgeon would enjoy ample opportunity to express his dependence on God, his absolute deference to grace, and how criticism and slander provided powerful prompts to rest only in the divine supply of strength.

A Theology of Slander

Slander may have a sanctifying influence. From the first day of his Christian life, Spurgeon longed for more rapid and more thorough sanctification. On 19 September 1850, he wrote his father to this effect: 'Yes, where Jesus comes, He comes to reign; how I wish He would reign more in my heart; then I might hope that every atom of self, self-confidence, and self-righteousness, would be swept out of my soul.' Not only self-confidence, but 'evil affections, corrupt desires, and rebellious, doubting thoughts' must be crushed if one is to become 'pure and holy'. The Spirit's work against indwelling sin operates to remove these latter operations of the flesh. The slaying of 'self-confidence and self-righteousness' can be helped along by the public observations, even if unfairly presented, of others. In God's purpose, not only fair and candid criticisms are helps along the way, but slander may be a helpful rasp to unwieldy self-centered edges. Slander, malice, and envy may drive the Christian to self-investigation, to an awareness of how easily destroyed are sensational first-impressions, and how truly zealous we must be for the glory of God alone.

Slander presents us with the opportunity to imitate Christ. In his commentary on Matthew, Spurgeon reminded the reader that 'The scholar is not more excellent than the teacher, nor the servant than his master.' If we are treated as our Master was treated 'we ought to be well content', for we have more honor in such an imitation than we have a right to expect. If Jesus was likened to '*Beelzebub*, the fly-god of the Philistines, and named after the prince of demons, by what names will they call us?' We should not melt then when malice quickens with and sarcasm invents 'words which pierce as daggers, and cut like knives.' The attribution of blasphemy to Jesus did not make Him a blasphemer. Evil names cannot make us evil. 'They can, and will cast out our names as evil, for they call good evil, and evil good.' Even so, is it not the height of irony that 'God was slandered in Paradise, and Christ on Calvary'? Should we hope to escape? Do not wish to avoid the cross but take it up and endure it for the sake of Christ. 'Let it be our ambition to be *as our Master* in all things.' Being of the household of Christ makes it the greatest of honors and the most auspicious of opportunities to be like the Master of the household. 'No price is too high to pay in consequence. Close conformity to the image of their Lord is the glory of saints.' For the servant to become as the master is the 'climax of his ambition'.

Slander may help us look forward to the day of impartial judgment. Continuing in his commentary on Matthew, Spurgeon reflected on chapter 10:26: 'Therefore do not fear them. For there is nothing covered that will not be revealed, and hidden that will not be known' (NKJV). Jesus encouraged His servants concerning harsh and unjust criticism, reminding them that the religious leaders had called Him Beelzebub. How much more susceptible would His servants be to such aspersions. 'The King gives reasons for courage, saying, "*Fear them not therefore.*"' Spurgeon drove the point to the specific situation Jesus was addressing, a point existentially powerful in his experience. 'Have no fear of slander; your Lord and Master bore the full blast of that pitiless storm. Have no fear of misrepresentation, for the great God will right your characters before long.' A judgment is coming, when in the investigation conducted by the impartial judge, 'You and your traducers will alike be shown up in the colours of truth.' Perhaps he took liberties with the immediate meaning of the text but certainly made a pertinent application when he wrote, 'Though you should be *covered* with obloquy, your integrity shall be *revealed*; though your true value is *hid,* it shall yet be *known*.' Spurgeon was sure that 'Secret villainy and secret virtue will alike be set in the full blaze of day'. A purpose of slander in its various degrees and manifestations, therefore, was to point us to the final verdict of the One who judges justly. 'Anticipate the future, and be not overwhelmed by the present.'[2]

Slander helps us relinquish claim to personal effectuality and glory in order to boast only in the Lord. By 1856, Spurgeon could look back at just over a year of public ministry in London. He had stirred reaction as varied as the weather of an English spring. 'I have been delighted to find myself abused as ignorant, unlearned, and void of eloquence,' Spurgeon noted. He knew this long before his critics. Though this could be fuel for pity and depression – and sometimes was – Spurgeon took it as evidence of the inexplicable blessing of God on his ministry. 'All the glory belongs to God,' for, fool that he was, he had become a 'fool in glorying'. He welcomed any opprobrious title that the world could sling at him, but 'they cannot deny the fact that God blesses my ministry, that harlots have been saved, that drunkards have been reclaimed, that some of the most abandoned characters have been changed.' Critics scowl. They love to count his appeal to the low-minded and cultural outcasts as an indication of his lack of learning, his lack of sophistication. He does not try to convince them otherwise, for 'God has wrought such a work in their midst as they never saw before in their lives. Therefore, give all the glory to His holy name.' He encouraged the worldlings to cast on him as much reproach as they liked, for then all the room is left for God alone to receive the glory. He alone 'worketh as he pleaseth, and with what instrument he chooseth, irrespective of men.'[3]

The Persistence of Slanderous Opposition

On the sixth anniversary of his conversion, 6 January 1856, Spurgeon preached on sovereignty and salvation. He used Isaiah 45:22, the passage that brought him to Christ and entered inextricably into his evangelistic vocabulary – 'Look to Jesus!' and his only confidence of

---

2. Commentary on *Matthew*, pp. 72, 73.
3. SEE 5:465.

success: 'For I am God and there is no other.' To the New Park Street congregation who knew of the wildly varied responses of London to their still-new pastor, Spurgeon gave them assurance that God was showing zeal for the glory of His name. There is an antidote to human conceit in matters of divine action that God applies especially to ministers: 'He raises up a host of enemies, that it may be seen that He is God, and God alone.' Referring to Whitefield as an example of one who endured severe ridicule and opposition for his conviction that salvation was wholly of God and for his insistence of preaching a God-glorifying message, he exclaimed: 'What! Will a man subject himself to the calumnies of the multitude, will he toil and work day after day un-necessarily, will he stand up Sabbath after Sabbath and preach the gospel and have his name maligned and slandered, if he has not the grace of God in him?'

Knowing his own disposition toward despondency combined with his inflexible zeal for truth, Spurgeon told them: 'For myself, I can say, that were it not that the love of Christ constrained me, this hour might be the last that I should preach, so far as the ease of the thing is concerned.' Such opposition, one must conclude, God brings about in leading His servants to see 'at once that he is God, and that there is none else.' If the minister were met with universal approbation and applause, if the whole world felt gratified with the message, self-satisfaction would give him a God-complex, but when they hiss and hoot we turn to our God, and cry,

> If on my face, for thy dear name,
> Shame and reproach should be,
> I'll hail reproach and welcome shame,
> If thou'lt remember me.[4]

Again in 1856, in preaching on the work of the Spirit in the covenant, Spurgeon said: 'Sometimes my heart has been shaken by disgrace, shame and contempt, for many a brother minister, of whom I

---

4. SS 1:12, 13.

thought better things, has reviled me.' Then accumulated disgrace came, for others believed the report and 'many a Christian has turned on his heels away from me because I had been misrepresented to him and he has hated me without a cause.' The comforting ministry of the Spirit, however, encouraged Spurgeon, and, in the midst of the storm of criticism, the quiet conviction given by the Spirit came, 'I am my Beloved's and my Beloved is mine.' Should the entire church turn its back and the whole world hiss at him, 'it would not have greatly moved me, for some bright ray of spiritual sunshine lit up my heart' in the form of those words of assurance. 'At such times the consolations of the Spirit have been neither few nor small with me!'[5] He wanted others to know those secret and personal ministries of the Spirit to the Christian.

In January 1857, in the preface to his second series published in America, Spurgeon again showed how criticism gave an opportunity to magnify God's grace. 'If these truths were only found united with a learned and eloquent ministry, they would be imputed to *the man*, and not to *the truth*,' he explained. His enemies, therefore, become strong witnesses that his success is all of grace. 'God hath put His treasure in earthen vessels, that the excellency of the power might be ascribed wholly to himself.' Spurgeon confessed the element of truth that was in every note of disparagement toward him, 'for therein we do but magnify the grace of God, who worketh by the least of instruments the greatest acts of His love.' He believed his ministry was a testimony to the power of undiluted truth proclaimed in the confidence that the Holy Spirit would bless the Word. 'O for the days of pure doctrine, preached with emphasis of earnestness, and demonstration of the Spirit; for these we look and wait. May the Lord send them in his own time.'[6]

Early in 1859 Spurgeon looked upon the difficulties he encountered when he first came to London as an opportunity for

---

5. MTP 53:3048 entitled 'The Holy Spirit in the Covenant.' www.spurgeongems. org

6. SS 2:vii.

Christian resignation. Thinking he could bear anything for Christ he found himself 'shamefully slandered' with 'all manner of falsehoods' being uttered against him. 'In agony I fell on my face before God,' Spurgeon recalled, and lamented remorsefully the falsehoods created to attack his character. It came to him, however, that all that was dear to him he must surrender to Christ – 'character, reputation, and all that you have.' If God willed that he be reckoned among 'vilest of the vile', while continuing to serve Him and having the knowledge that 'your character is really pure', then he need not fear. He came to a place of joyful resignation of willingness to be 'trampled and spat upon by all the wicked men in the world', bearing it according to the will of God.[7]

In July 1859, he preached on God's Mighty Acts, and queried if God intended to use the agency of the Surrey Gardens Music Hall for the conversion of those who heard him. Perhaps groans of true repentance, instead of injury, would be heard in the Hall. He was happy to think that such could be the case but felt sure that none should place any dependence upon the instrument. 'No,' he assured, 'when men laughed at us and mocked us most, God blessed us most. And now, it is not a disreputable thing to attend the Music Hall.' He was not as despised as once he was, but he questioned 'whether we have as great a blessing as we once had'. For the sake of souls he would be 'willing to endure another pelting in the stocks; to go through another ordeal with every newspaper against us and with every man hissing and abusing us, if God so pleases.' If that were the cost of a blessing, so let it be. 'Only let Him cast out of us any idea that our own bow and sword will get us victory! We shall never get a revival here unless we believe that it is the Lord, and the Lord alone, who can do it!'[8]

The minister of the gospel should beware, in fact, of applause from the world. 'A Christian minister may go on preaching very

---

7. SEE 14:475.
8. NPSP 5. 'The Story of God's Mighty Acts,' www.spurgeongems.org

earnestly, and God will help him, though everybody opposes him.' When he gets pats on the back, however, and he becomes pleased in being seen as a fine fellow and a great man, he must realize that a true test of faithfulness is on its way. Soon the world will seek to blunt the witness and the commitment to truth that God blessed. Soon he will be tempted to enjoy the fine opinion of the world and will round off the sharp edges of truth. In such a time, he must realize that 'the friendship of the world is as much enmity with God as it used to be in apostolic times'. If the 'courtier is in great favor with the king's enemies', it is no good sign. Under the power of this temptation, the preacher must stand out as a man of God 'whether you offend or please'. Faith will flourish and usefulness increase when one survives the trial of applause.[9]

By 1877, Spurgeon had not escaped the culture of criticism, for some heavily-spiced anecdote about him was always good to sell a pamphlet, make a cartoon, or sell a paper. He had grown so accustomed to it, however, and had so embraced the reality as part of the cost he must pay for transparent faithfulness to Christ, the Bible, and the conversion of sinners, that his sensitivities had transcended the murky flow of publicity. Still, however, he knew that without a constantly renewed affection for the glory of Christ above all earthly expectations, the lure of worldly likeability could be compelling. On the evening of 7 January, he preached on 'The Saddest Cry from the Cross'. Engaged in some of the most closely reasoned theological exposition in the Spurgeon corpus, Spurgeon discussed, 'My God, my God, why has thou forsaken me?' Having affirmed all the elements of Christ's person and holy love for the Father that contributed to the power of His vicarious death for sinners, Spurgeon reminded his hearers 'that the doctrine of substitution is the key to all the sufferings of Christ'. By way of application, Spurgeon asserted that, in light of such suffering for the salvation of sinners and the glory of God, 'Let us be ready to suffer

---

9. NPSP 5. 'The Story of God's Mighty Acts,' www.spurgeongems.org

anything for His sake.' Even should we lose all the joy of religion in the process, we should endure it if it would glorify God. Perhaps we should be like Moses and be willing to have our names blotted out of the Book of Life for the sake of God's name. If not pressed to such an extreme, still 'Let us be willing to lose our reputation'. Spurgeon reminded his hearers, 'Some of us,' – a favorite phrase of Spurgeon when referring to his own experience – 'when we first came into public notice and found our words picked to pieces – and our character slandered – felt it rather difficult.' Now, however, he had adjusted to it, 'but it was very trying at first.' Looking at what Christ endured, how He was forsaken of God for us, we should gladly endure the epithet of 'Devil', be willing to 'be spat upon by every passer-by' and take up that cross 'with thankfulness that we were permitted to bear it!'[10]

He That Endureth to the End

In the final analysis, temptations to consider the safety of self above the glory of the cross come from Satan, the arch-enemy of redemption and the enemy of our souls. To endure so much through many years but to fail finally would be tragic indeed. Spurgeon illustrated that the instigator of all attacks upon faithfulness to the redeeming love of Christ was Satan himself. He reported an interview with a former pastor of the Metropolitan Tabernacle, James Smith, whom he had visited during a sickness. Smith had spoken at the dedication of the Tabernacle in April 1861 and soon after was struck with paralysis, a massive stroke, and, in Spurgeon's words, 'one half of his body was dead.'

In spite of that, Spurgeon's visit found a man filled with as much joy as if he had been in the most potent time of youth. Spurgeon had heard that Smith had times of 'doubts and fears'. 'Who told you that?' Smith responded, 'for I have none.' He had experienced conflicts of

---

10. 'The Saddest Cry from the Cross,' *A Treasury of Spurgeon on the Life and Work of our Lord,* 6:553, 554.

mind but never any doubts. He had wars but not fears. He hoped he had not given any impression of doubts, for his conflicts came from a desire to die quickly and be with Christ, but the time was delayed day by day. 'It is a hard battle, but I know the victory is sure,' he reported. 'After I have had an ill night's rest – of course, through physical debility – my mind is troubled, and then, that old coward, Satan, who would be afraid to meddle with me, perhaps, if I were strong, attacks me when I am weak.' But he was unafraid of Satan no matter how many fiery darts he threw. Then Smith said: 'I am just like a packet that is all ready to go by train, packed, corded, labeled, paid for, and on the platform, waiting for the express to come by and take me to Glory. I wish I could hear the whistle now.' He wanted heaven long ago, but he was so fixed to the Rock that unless the Rock falls, he cannot. 'Unless the Gospel perishes, I cannot perish.'

Spurgeon then applied Smith's testimony to the testimony all Christians must bear against the slander of Satan. 'Now, here was a man attacked by Satan – he did not tell me of the bitter conflicts he had within, I know they were severe enough, but he was anxious to bear a good testimony to the faithfulness of his gracious Lord.' God was his stronghold and he ran to a personal conviction of the attributes of God – 'the Immutability, the Faithfulness, the Truthfulness, the Mightiness of that God upon whose arm he leaned!' So must we learn to do the same.

> 'God will leave you,' says the Evil One. 'You old liar, He cannot, for He is a faithful God.' 'But you will perish after all.' 'O you vile deceiver! That can never be, for He is a mighty God and strong to deliver.' 'But one of these times, He will abhor you.' 'No, you false accuser, and father of lies, that cannot be, for He is a God of Love.' 'The time shall happen when He shall forget you.' 'No, traitor! That cannot be, for He is a God Omniscient, and knows and sees all things.' I say, thus, we may rebut every mischievous slander of Satan, running still into the Character of God as our strong tower![11]

---

11. MTP 9:491: 'Our Stronghold.'

When we learn to refute the slander of Satan against God, we will be prepared to see the wiliness of the fiend in the criticism and slander of others toward us. When our testimony to the established truth of God derived from His inspired Word is under attack in our personal witness, we surely can see an assault on the glory of God.

In significant ways, a barrage of criticism received late in his ministry was different from what Spurgeon experienced in his early years in London. Then he received criticism and ridicule partly because he espoused the doctrines of grace, but mainly over such issues as his youth, his confidence interpreted as impudence, his love of the Puritans, his diminished accomplishments in formal education, and his popularity interpreted as Mountebankism (simplistic answers to complex problems for self-indulgent and financially profitable reasons). Late in his ministry, his continuation in historic orthodoxy, as well as evangelical Calvinism, prompted public scorn from some leading religious publications like *The Christian World,* and from the school of advanced thinkers among the clergy. Perhaps most bitterly, the Downgrade controversy had put Spurgeon in tension with many of his friends in the Baptist Union. Spurgeon had resigned from the Baptist Union in October 1887. The Union Council had published what amounted to a censure of Spurgeon in January 1888. In addition, during February 1888, Spurgeon was in the process of dissolving the Pastors' College Conference in order to reorganize it on a stronger confessional basis. He hoped that all of the alumni in love with modern thought would be honest enough not to sign the confession and simply leave him as 'an immovable old man'. Spurgeon remained unintimidated and just as resolute as before. In February 1888 he preached on the words of Jesus to the church at Pergamos. The subject was 'Holding Fast the Faith'. Again, his grasp of the glory of Christ and the power of grace steeled him for the conflict. He said that one element of holding fast the faith was a love for the name of Jesus and maintaining its infinite dignity 'in the teeth of all opposition'. We must dash to the front of the battle when the name is assaulted. 'Ease, reputation, life itself, must go for the name and faith of Jesus.' With a willingness to lose all for the glory of the name, Spurgeon called on his hearers to join him and 'take part and lot with my Master, and bear reproach for his sake.' Cowards may sneak to the rear, seek comfort, and acceptance, and commendation, but true lovers of the name 'must be willing to bear ridicule for Christ's sake, even that peculiarly envenomed ridicule which "the cultured" are so apt to pour upon us.' He claimed to have forgotten more than his opponents knew and yet he was branded as ignorant; he bore shame out of the courage of conviction, yet was hounded as a coward. Jesus ascended to His throne by a cross, but some seem to think they will be 'carried there on the shoulders of applauding crowds'. He had a word of seasoned warning: 'Be not so vain in your imagination.'[12]

Spurgeon had a goal in his Pastors' College to train men to be sound in doctrine, earnest in conviction, clear in proclamation, and without compromise in the conflict of truth with error. His reorganization of the conference showed his resolute commitment to that purpose. If he were successful in that, then he also would need to prepare them for standing during days of conflict and in the presence of insult, misrepresentation, and abuse. His personal experience informed his instructions on this issue. In a message to his men at the College, Spurgeon, during the Downgrade controversy, gave some insight as to how he was enabled to withstand criticism and attempts to make him soften his representation of the destructive dangers of error. 'I am content with that which must inevitably come to the man who protests in downright earnest,' he told the men; 'that is to say, I am content to be criticized, misunderstood, and misrepresented. The cost was counted long ago, and the estimate was so liberal that there is no fear of its being exceeded.'[13] Expectations eliminate the element of surprise and thus minimize distress.

---

12. SS 19:44, 45.
13. *An All Round Ministry*, p. 395.

In July 1888, Spurgeon stood astounded that God used weak men as a subordinate means in effecting the covenant of redemption. Controversy, criticism, and fatigue on the one hand with apostasy, doctrinal infidelity, and human fickleness on the other, Spurgeon wondered that any positive advance was made at all. 'To work by men must bring special glory to God,' Spurgeon observed. 'The weaker the instrument,' men in all their troubles, 'the more honor to the worker,' the triune God in His sovereign immutability. The Lord 'shall conquer by feeble men even to the end'. Even as the Lord used fishermen, tax-collectors, and persecutors, 'If the Lord will graciously use us poor ministers to the end, it will wonderfully illustrate His wisdom and power.' The divinity of Christianity is proved in that it has survived its ministers. He wondered how his congregation had survived him and how the whole gospel had survived its advocates, poor fools and poor tools, 'specially myself.' Given such weak vessels, the Lord 'must certainly have all the glory of it'.[14]

In 1891 at the height of the Downgrade controversy and very near the time of Spurgeon's last sermon, he recognized that his position was presented as antiquated, unenlightened, and brittle; and he was seen personally as divisive and unbrotherly in his separatistic stance. For Spurgeon, however, the cause did not finally center on him, but on divine truth. From the beginning to the end of his ministry, he had been willing to take the apostolic abuse as the off-scouring of the world if he also could enjoy the apostolic confidence of having kept the faith. 'We are a set of pigmies – it is all right if He is exalted! God's Truth is safe.' Spurgeon assured his church of his willingness 'to be forgotten, derided, slandered, or anything else that men please,' for he had determined that 'the cause is safe and the King is on the Throne. Hallelujah! Blessed be His name!'[15]

---

14. MTP 34:2032: 'The Charge of the Angel.' www.spurgeongems.org
15. MTP 37:2213: 'Honey in the Mouth!' www.spurgeongems.org

10

'BLESSED BIBLE! THOU ART ALL TRUTH'

• • • • • • • • • • • • • • • • • • • •

In the month of his conversion, January 1850, Spurgeon wrote his father, 'How beautiful is the Bible! I never loved it so before; it seems to me as necessary food.'[1] Spurgeon's commitment to Scripture began and remained the final touchstone in all of these other parts of ministry and personal life. This tenacious adherence created a habit of independence of judgment that was startling, refreshing, maddening, perplexing, and enraging to his contemporary churchmen and Christian thinkers.

One that dared dismiss Scripture as erroneous in any part not only attacked the veracity and reign of God but slit his own throat. He left himself without light from above to guide into the treacherous shoals of death regnant with the wrath of God apart from the ransom to which Scripture alone bears witness. It is the book that God wrote and to deny it is to charge God with error. Preaching in March 1855, in considering all its varied penmen, Spurgeon looked at their unanimous testimony to the revelation of God and concluded: 'This volume is the writing of the living God – each letter was penned with an Almighty finger. Each word in it dropped from the everlasting lips, each sentence was dictated by the

---

1. Murray, *Letters*, p. 20.

Holy Spirit.' Spurgeon, therefore, felt fully warranted to proclaim, 'This is the book untainted by any error!' but like its author was 'pure unalloyed, perfect truth.'[2] Thus his own judgment was freed from the oppressiveness of human opinion and the shifting theologies of modern thought. Even the inherited traditional theologies of the past were not exempt from passing biblical muster.

Prince of the Intellect

In 'Sovereignty and Salvation', Spurgeon compared the trans-temporal truthfulness of Scripture to the temporary systems of thought devised by the highly-touted wise men of the world. He looked at the systems of Aristotle, Solon, Bacon, and any 'new sect of philosophers' who rise up to 'refute their predecessors'. 'Systems of infidelity,' as he called these secularist attempts at defining truth, 'pass away like a dew-drop before the sun.' But the Bible! – every Abimelech should fear it as the stone that will crush his head, for it is a 'stone that shall break in powder philosophy', and it is the 'battering ram that shall dash all systems of philosophy in pieces'.[3]

Spurgeon relates something of his understanding of the integration of human giftedness with divine inspiration in speaking of the text, 'The carnal mind is enmity against God' (Rom. 8:7 NKJV). He encouraged his hearers to 'weigh the words of the text, for they are solemn words.' On the one hand, they deserve such attention because 'they are well put together by that master of eloquence, Paul.' Beyond that, however, as is the case in all of Scripture, they were 'dictated by the Holy Spirit, who telleth man how to speak aright.'[4]

Divine revelation triumphs over philosophy and reason both in the importance and the certainty of its subject matter. Spurgeon argued, concerning the doctrine of original sin, that though every aspect of human existence witnesses to it, 'It needs no proof, for since it is written in God's Word, we, as Christian men, are bound

---

2. SS 1:31
3. SS 1:9
4. SS 1:233.

to bow before it.' As a matter of divine revelation, the propositions of Scripture needed no independent verification for their truthfulness, for the 'words of the Scriptures are words of infinite wisdom, and if reason cannot see the ground of a statement of revelation, it is bound, most reverently, to believe it, since we are well assured, even should it be above our reason, that it cannot be contrary thereunto.'[5]

Spurgeon found the knowledge of Christ and Him crucified as presented and explained in the Bible to be the key of intellectual attainment and worldview coherence. 'I confess I have a shelf in my head for everything now,' he revealed. 'Whatever I read I know where to put it, whatever I learn I know where to stow it away.' Formerly the reading of books only resulted in 'glorious confusion', but knowledge of Christ organized his mind. 'I have put Christ in the center as my sun, and each science revolves round it like a planet, while minor sciences are satellites to these planets.' All true wisdom – the wisdom of God Himself – is found in Christ with the result that 'I can learn everything now. The science of Christ crucified is the most excellent of sciences, she is to me the wisdom of God.' He thus appealed with confidence to young men to build their studio on Calvary and there raise their observatory. They should find their hermit's cell in Gethsemane and lave their brows 'with the waters of Siloam'. The biblical picture of the person of Christ as foundational to the work of Christ is unsurpassed in any literature and infinitely superior to the hazy guesses of the philosophers. 'Let the Bible be your standard classic – your last appeal in matters of contention. Let its light be your illumination, and you shall become more wise than Plato, more truly learned than the seven sages of antiquity.'[6]

Unblemished Perfection

Spurgeon never shifted from his full confidence in the inspiration of the Bible and the power of proclaiming it without hesitation

---

5. SS 1:234.
6. SS 1:109, 110.

or reservation. In 1880, preaching to his students in the college, Spurgeon affirmed his certainty that 'the book which is called "the Bible" is His Word, and is inspired.' All of it is to be received as God's sure testimony and nothing less than that. We should not be ensnared by the subtleties of those who would diminish this certainty by musing in print about a variety of modes of inspiration in a way that fritters away our certainty. Spurgeon was keenly tuned in to a variety of accusations concerning 'bibliolatry' toward those who believed in the infallibility of Scripture. These kinds of sneers showed both their misunderstanding of the real belief of the inerrantist as well as a snobbish disregard for the glory of the Bible's author. Those who accept the Scriptures as infallible would to a man declare that they do not worship the book, but adore its author. 'The book is a divine production; it is perfect, and is the last court of appeal.... I would as soon dream of blaspheming my Maker as of questioning the infallibility of His Word.'[7]

In an article entitled 'Remarks on Inspiration', Spurgeon identified 'The turning point of the battles between those who hold "the faith once delivered to the saints" and their opponents' as 'the true and real inspiration of the Holy Scriptures'. It is the 'Thermopylae of Christendom'. The entire battle for truth turns on it. 'If we have in the Word of God no infallible standard of truth, we are at sea without a compass.' The Christian minister 'must part company altogether with the errorist, who overrides prophets and apostles, and practically regards his own inspiration as superior to theirs.'[8]

The infallibility of Scripture involves not only the mental reception of its doctrinal propositions, but the personal appropriation of its promises. One may be quick in receiving scriptural teaching on the deity of Christ, substitutionary atonement and other gospel doctrines but be tardy in embracing comfort. In the same way that the disciples on the Emmaus road were slow to believe all that the

---

7. *Lectures*, 2:41.
8. S&T, May 1888:20.

Scripture said, though they had all the evidence in the correlation of recent events with clear prophecy, so are we slow to believe God's promises. Mark you, not hard of heart toward the volume of inspiration, but slow of heart. Those devout Jews 'accepted the Holy Books as divinely inspired, and therefore infallible,' but acted as if they did not believe the prophets. 'Are we not often found guilty of like inconsistency?' It is one thing to say, 'I believe the Bible,' and quite another to have confidence and courage on the basis of that belief. 'Let us have our wits about us,' Spurgeon urged, 'and make serious business of that which is not sent to delude us, but to instruct us.' God's Word is in harmony with His providence, and, if we trust Him in the one, we should be sure to trust Him in the other. We must not believe man in his schemes, threats, and deceits, but 'accept every syllable of God's Word as infallible'. We must not only believe in God for eternity but also for bread and cheese. We believe the false comforts of fallible men, 'Yet the incorruptible Word is mistrusted.' Often our slowness comes because we do not know enough of Scripture. 'A want of familiarity with the Word of God is very often the seed-plot of our doubts.' Also, lack of care in comparing God's providence in our lives with the promises of His Word robs us of the comfort of confirmation. The blessing of an infallible Word for the disturbed soul may be an equal blessing to those of the saving truths of the gospel. 'When you see more of what God has revealed,' Spurgeon spoke as one experienced in desponding spirits, 'you will rise out of your doubts and fears, and your slowness of heart to believe will depart from you.'[9]

Scripture in its relation to Systematic Theology

Spurgeon did not want the thirst for organization to cloud the exuberant richness of God's Word by seeking to reduce everything to a system or a shape. Though he commended John Gill for 'good, sound, massive, sober sense in commenting,' he did find fault

---

9. SS 18:309, 315, 319.

with him at this very point. Though he is most often chaste in his contextual exegesis of Scripture, even challenging texts, sometimes 'he falls upon a text which is not congenial with his creed, and hacks and hews terribly to bring the Word of God into a more systematic shape.'[10]

If such an organizational feat were possible, Spurgeon was convinced that 'No man who has yet lived has ever proposed a system of theology which comprises all the truth of God's Word'. If a fuller richness and power profitable for holiness could be given by 'a system of theology which comprises all the truth of God's Word', then God Himself certainly would have given it.[11] Instead, Spurgeon looked at the book of God much like the works of God, 'not systematically arranged.' The freedom of nature is far different from the British Museum where all the animals are 'placed in cases according to their respective orders'. Animals do not roam in such ordered closed cases nor are rocks 'laid in order as the geologist draws them in his books'. The stars of the heavens are not 'marked off according to their magnitudes'.

Even so, variety and admixture of the sweet and sour, the plain and the difficult, the transparent and the cloudy, dominate Scripture. None need be lost in the depth of an argument in Scripture, for difficult ideas and passages are surrounded with the clear and plain. The man at the plow as well as the scholar at his table may find spiritual richness in each part. 'It is a primer for babes, as well as a classic for sages. It is the humble, ignorant man's book.' Though resident throughout it are depths 'in which the elephant may swim', yet in the same places 'are shallows where the lamb may wade'. As a 'handbook to Heaven' and a 'guide to eternity', we are thankful that God has not 'given us a body of divinity in which we might lose ourselves'. Instead He has given His Word in 'the very best practical form for our daily use and edification!' We should, therefore, receive

---

10. *Lectures*, 4:9.
11. SEE 15:174. Sermon entitled 'The Sweetness of God's Word'.

and savor all that He has given, 'each truth in its own proportion, – each doctrine in harmony with its fellow, – each precept carefully carried out and put into practice, and each promise to be believed, and by-and-by received.'[12]

At the same time, Spurgeon recognized the value and interpretive power of systematic arrangement of data, whether natural or revealed. After all, he did commend the conviction that would seek 'each truth in its own proportion, each doctrine in harmony with its fellow.' 'Science,' he observed, 'does but arrange and classify, so as to assist the memory.' In the same way, when the systematic divine finds 'Scriptural Truths put, not in order for the classroom, but for common life,' he plays the useful part of the 'analytical chemist, or the anatomist.' While recognizing that 'the Bible is not arranged as a body of divinity', he sees that due to its consistency and non-contradictory character it is capable of coherent and connected arrangement of its varied propositions.[13]

Though Spurgeon gloried in laying out the truths of the Bible as they appeared in their context, he nevertheless benefited in his own exposition by a thorough knowledge of both historical and systematic theology. In preaching on sanctification, he introduced the idea by reminding his auditors, 'In deeds of divine grace none of the persons of the Trinity act apart from the rest. They are as united in their deeds as in their essence.'[14] His knowledge of Nicene orthodoxy and the idea of *circumincessio* aided him in that introductory thought.

In a sermon on 'Trust in the Living God', Spurgeon discussed the concept of 'living' under six categories that showed his own propensity to systematize biblical ideas, expanding both natural and moral attributes into a configuration of compelling beauty and power. Without the language of art, nevertheless, he spoke of God's eternity, omnipotence, aseity, simplicity, immensity, immanence,

---

12. SEE, 15:174.
13. MTP 8:434: 'Threefold Sanctification'.
14. Ibid.

transcendence, immutability, impassibility, wisdom, holiness, love, wrath, righteousness, and mercy, saying along the way,

> We have no independent immortality; it is not inherent in us, and it must be sustained by perpetual emanations of the divine power. ... God is independent, self-existing, the only really "living" being in the entire universe. ... God is all alive, and altogether life, and nothing but life. God's wisdom is always infallible, His power is always almighty, His energy is at all times efficacious for everything that needs His attention. There never can come a time when He will be bowed down with age, or wearied with toil, or affected by suffering ... a God with a great warm, loving heart, a thinking God, an active God, a working personal God, who comes into the midst of this world, and does not leave it to go on by itself.[15]

Only a commitment to perfect consistency, unalloyed truthfulness, and revelatory perfection can foster such a confident series of propositions about God. While the Bible defied an exhaustive systematization, only the Bible could generate the attempt to deduce such a discussion of divine attributes.

Every Word Is Important

There is nothing in God's Bible which is not great and no word that is not important. Spurgeon commended the regular practice of commenting on twenty or more verses during every public meeting, for otherwise some parts of God's Word would never enter the mind of most people. 'If you want to make full proof of your ministry,' he encouraged, 'and to leave no single point of revelation untouched, your easiest mode will be to comment upon Scripture habitually.'[16]

As he asked his hearers concerning their duty to seek the greatest purity in their situations of worship, he proposed the question, 'Did any of you ever sit down to see which was the purest religion?' Supposing that they had never taken the trouble but merely followed

---

15. SEE 15:21-28.
16. *Lectures*, 4:23.

their parents, he chided, 'Ah, that is a profound reason, indeed! You went where your father and mother did. I thought you were sensible people.' He related that though he loved his parents above all breathing things, and looked upon their convictions as a great impetus to accept their truthfulness, he said, 'But I have not followed them – I belong to a different denomination – and I thank God I do.' In that context he argued that every person should investigate the question for himself, paying close attention to the very words of Scripture and the biblical pattern of truth. 'Never say it doesn't matter. It does matter. Whatever God has put here is of eminent importance – He would not have written a thing that was indifferent.' All questions must be decided by the Word of God. He wanted every utterance of his to be tried by the Word of God, and if found to be in error, 'I will withdraw it the next Sunday.' Permit him a fair field and the Bible, investigate and criticize, but 'don't say, "It does not matter." If God says a thing, it must always be of importance.'[17]

Preaching on Ezekiel 40:4, 'Taught that we may Teach,' Spurgeon focused on the intensity with which God instructed Ezekiel to use all his powers of sight, hearing, and thinking to observe 'everything I show you', so that he would be able to 'declare to the house of Israel everything you see'. Ezekiel was to listen with all his might. Spy out every meaning with the mind's eye and 'try to catch the very tone in which the promise or precept has been uttered'. God gave instructions to 'treasure up the exact words, for though cavilers call it folly to speak of verbal Inspiration, I believe that we must have verbal Inspiration or no Inspiration.' Should one say that he was communicating the sense of what one's father had instructed, the reply should be, 'Yes, but I would like to know precisely what he said, word for word.' In legal documents, such is the case. It is not merely the sense that one should look for, as if that could be determined with precision apart from the exact words, 'but every word must be correct.' Language is of such a nature that 'God's

17. SS 1:37.

Word, as it came from Him, came in such perfection that even to the syllables in which the sense was clothed, there was Infallibility about it.' Like Ezekiel in response to the Lord's instruction, 'When I get God's Word I would desire to hear it with my ears as well as see it with my eyes – to see its sense and then to love the expressions in which that sense is conveyed to me!' It is doubtful if one cares intensely for 'the sense of the words who is not jealous over the words which convey the sense!'

The Bible conveys the opening of the heart of God to His people. Each must take care not to lose anything. 'Do not lose a sound – a syllable!' Even more than that, set your heart upon it. We only learn truly by 'loving all that He says – feeling that whatever God says, it is the thing you need to know.' The whole heart must look to God's truth and encompass 'it about with warm affections so that it may be like a fly in amber, the Word in the midst of your heart – encased there, enshrined there – never to be taken away from you!'

Though reading large sections of Scripture is good, and Spurgeon encouraged reading the entire Bible regularly, this must be done in the context of intense concentrated study of the Word. 'I would rather lay my soul soaking in half a dozen verses all day than I would, as it were, rinse my hands in several chapters,' Spurgeon advised. 'Oh, to bathe in a text of Scripture and to let it be sucked up into your very soul till it saturates your heart!' In the same way that the 'man who has read many books is not always a learned man', but rather the one who has mastered three or four, so must we set our hearts on God's Word, and let our 'whole nature be plunged into it as cloth into dye. The Lord bids us do this towards all that He shall show us – "set your heart upon all that I shall show you!"'

Even so, passages that are difficult or that challenge our assumptions must be studied with care and submission. 'We are to be impartial in our study of the Word of God and to be universal in its reception.' Set aside all other reading until that one passage that displeases you is set with force and beauty in your conscience. 'Learn to love it for if there is a quarrel between you and a Scripture, it is you that is wrong, not the Scripture!' The Word of God will never change, so if you differ from it, 'the party to change is yourself!' Even in the challenge to one's favorite sentiments or leading to the necessity of changing denominations, the Bible must be followed fully. '"Are we to be so particular in little things?" asks one. Yes, it is in little things that loyalty comes. A loving and obedient child obeys his father without saying, "This is a great thing and this is a little thing."'[18]

Every Word Is Sweet

God's words to the believer are 'sweet to us as a whole – when we love the truth, not cast into a system or a shape, but as we find it in God's Word.'[19] Seeing it as the Word of Christ to his soul, Spurgeon considered Scripture as his peace, his strength, his life, his motive, his hope, his happiness. 'God's Word is our ultimatum,' he declared. His understanding cried, 'I have found it,' and his conscience asserted, 'Here is the truth; and our heart finds here a support to which all her affections can cling; and hence we rest content.'[20]

Like Jonathan Edwards, an ocean and a century away, Spurgeon believed that the Bible commended itself, by the Spirit, to a person's affections, or sensibilities, in such a way that its truthfulness and power attached itself with a virtual empirical certainty to the heart. False philosophy falls to the ground for the Christian who has tasted the sweetness of the Word, even as it is vain for a skeptic to say that honey is not sweet to the one who has just put a spoonful in his mouth. 'I should laugh in his face when I had once got the sweetness of it on my palate.'[21]

> No infidel or skeptical remark can have any power over your mind if you are at the present moment in the conscious enjoyment of the comfort and sweetness of God's Word. If you feel that it cheers you in the dark, what a fool he must be who says that it does not give you

---

18. *The Gospel for the People,* pp. 209-10.
19. SEE 15:174.
20. *The Greatest Fight in the World,* pp. 41, 42.
21. SEE 15:182.

light! Why, the man can have no toleration from you if he says it does not strengthen when you feel the strength of it.[22]

The Psalmist said, 'How sweet are Your words to my taste' (Ps. 119:103 NKJV). If it were so to the Psalmist, still under the ceremonial law and in the time of unfulfilled prophecy and the covenant promises still awaiting manifestation, yet more sweet should it be to us – and yet how far short do we fall from what seemed true of him. From God's mouth to our mouth, 'the blessedness of the Word is a matter to be ascertained by personal experience.'[23] This is not a matter of proxy or of hearing glowing testimony of the sweetness of God's Word, but it must be ascertained by dint of personal application. Every person must take and eat and feed himself; then we can say with Spurgeon, 'My palate shall be satisfied with thy Word, O God.'[24]

Nothing More Is Absolutely Needed

Spurgeon loved books. In his 'Catalogue of Biblical Commentaries & Expositions', he recommended 1,437 commentaries, including sixty-five on the whole Bible. He included short comments on each as to the peculiar strength, or weakness, of each volume. He listed forty-nine books of anecdotes and illustrations in addition to a large discussion of other books that would provide a variety of illustrations for the preacher.

He introduced his 'Chat About Commentaries' with the chastening admonition, 'You will need to be familiar with the commentators: a glorious army, let me tell you, whose acquaintance will be your delight and profit.' Then to add a bit of shame to any desire for utter independence in exposition, Spurgeon noted: 'Of course, you are not such wiseacres as to think or say that you can expound Scripture without assistance from the works of divines and learned men who have labored before you in the field of exposition.'[25]

---

22. Ibid.
23. SEE 15:174.
24. SEE 15:174.
25. Ibid.

Not only did he challenge ministers to read books and keep a steady flow of increased usefulness to the library shelves, he chided churches that would not make provision for the preacher's study-table as well as his dinner-table. Those who complain about poor sermons, and yet keep their minsters poor, should 'give over expecting to receive instructive sermons from men who are shut out of the storehouse of knowledge by their inability to purchase books.'[26]

Given that all-too-common situation, what are such men to do? He recommended that, in light of meager funds, the minister should purchase the very best, not 'milk and water, but get condensed milk.' Second, each should 'master those books that you have'. Become saturated with them, re-read them, digest them. The student will find that 'his mental condition is more affected by one book thoroughly mastered than by twenty books which he has merely skimmed.' Third, the one with slender apparatus can do some 'judicious borrowing'. Read them quickly, but thoroughly and with careful note-taking, but be sure to return them. Then the lender will be more apt to permit more borrowing.[27]

Most importantly, however, the one book more valuable than all others is your Bible. Having the Bible with a determination to use it aptly is like David with his sling and stone, 'fully equipped for the fray.' The Bible is a 'perfect library, and he who studies it thoroughly will be a better scholar than if he had devoured the Alexandrian Library entire.' The minister should know everything about it – 'its general run, the contents of each book, the details of its histories, its doctrines, its precepts.'[28]

Spurgeon related facts of the great works of scholarship that were the result of very few extra books combined with a prodigious knowledge of all of Scripture. An old minister in Lancashire was known as a 'walking Concordance', for he could cite a verse from the mention of its location, or tell the location from a recitation

---

26. *Lectures*, 1:191.
27. *Lectures*, 1:192-94.
28. *Lectures*, 1:195.

of a verse. A man of one book is a dangerous man, a formidable antagonist. 'A man who has his Bible at his fingers' ends and in his heart's core is a champion in our Israel.' The best illustrations, anecdotes, images, and other figures of speech come from Scripture itself, and the sermon adorned with them in apt demonstration of a point has all the more power and advantage over the souls of the congregation.[29]

William Romaine, during his latter years, put away all his books but the Bible, a scholar dominated by that one book, who gained all the more power in the exchange. To be engulfed in Scripture alone will never rob its earnest devotee of holy matter for preaching, but will constantly enrich his soul, his thought, and his ministry of proclamation. The power and infinitely glorious content of the Bible, when pursued diligently and with intentional thought, can turn an apparent disadvantage into a great gift. The lack of books and the insights and gifts from others is not a situation necessarily to be coveted; but to the one willing to ponder, meditate, and think deeply about the revealed truth of God, the isolation of mind to that one book can transform the loss into great gain.[30]

What More Can He Say

Spurgeon pushed aside, not only philosophy and destructive critical assessments of Scripture, but extra-canonical revelations, which held no place in his wardrobe of divine instruction. The thoroughness, sweetness, and self-witness of Scripture convinced Spurgeon that one should not look for 'angels' visits, or miraculous signs, or officiating priesthoods, or special revelations,' but must find rest in 'the words of God's mouth, and in the testimonies of Holy Writ.'[31]

Giving an exposition to the Lord's words through Isaiah in 45:16-19, Spurgeon assured his hearers that 'there is nothing in the secret book of God's decrees, and nothing in the sealed book

---

29. *Lectures,* 1:196
30. *Lectures,* 1:196, 197.
31. SEE 15:171.

of prophecy, which is contrary to the gracious covenant promises which God has revealed to His people in His Word.' Though some speak of revelations yet to be given, if any such thing exists, they 'will never contradict what has been revealed of old'. When the 'poorest and meanest of His people' spell out from Scripture their title to eternal life they 'may rely upon it that, if any wise man comes to them with some wonderful discovery which contradicts the Bible, he simply comes with a lie, for God has nowhere contradicted what he has plainly revealed in the Scriptures.'[32]

Preaching on 1 Corinthians 13:10, 'when the perfect is come,' Spurgeon remarked about Paul's visions from God. Though God 'came to him in the visions of the night, we do not expect to see the Lord Jesus Christ in visions, now.' Why? Referring to the 'more sure Word of prophecy' in 2 Peter 1:19, Spurgeon affirmed, 'we have the Word of God, Inspired and Infallible! We have the whole of the Divinely written roll.' The canon is complete and we 'read it when we will and from its pages God speaks with a clear and certain voice.' Even when God spoke through dreams, still it might only be a dream, 'but this Word of the Lord is no delusion! It stands fast forever and ever and every promise is sure, being made yes and amen in Christ Jesus.' Promises of the Word received by faith provide the experience of Christ's speaking personally to each of us because the promise never ceases to be true. 'It is as fresh today, when I read it, as when the eyes of saints a thousand years ago found comfort in it!' The very thing that God told Paul in his vision in Corinth, the saint today may read and claim from Isaiah. 'Fear not, I am with you,' with this additional strong assurance: 'I am your God. When you go through the fire, you shall not be burned, neither shall the flame kindle upon you.' Visions were needed in the church's infancy. The Word is now complete, and the faith has been tested for generations. The richness of Scripture, its fulness, and its inexhaustibility renders further visions and revelations unnecessary. Nothing needs to be

---

32. SEE 7:310.

'supplemented by signs and wonders'. A young tree may need a stake for support, but 'Nobody thinks of putting a post to support an apple tree which has been there for the last fifty years!' A tow may pull a ship out of a dock and down the river, but when it reaches the sea the tow is a mere superfluity incapable of matching the majesty of the ship in full sail.

The Church of God is the tree that needs no support of miracles and visions! For two thousand years, she is a vessel that has braved the battle and will continue till Christ comes. 'O servants of Jesus, you have the Word of God, which is better than visions!'[33]

Firm to the End

In 1891 when Spurgeon preached at his final Pastors' College Conference, he chose the theme, *The Greatest Fight in the World*. Wearied, but also spiritually energized, by the Downgrade controversy, Spurgeon took his stand for an uncompromising loyalty to the Bible as the infallible Word of God. He informed his loyal graduates then of his resolution 'to use more fully than ever what God has provided for us in this Book, for we are sure of its inspiration.' He repeated the conviction: 'WE ARE SURE OF ITS INSPIRATION.' He pointed out that the current intellectual trend in theology was to aim at the supposed absurdity of 'verbal inspiration'. He saw this as a mere pretext for denying any kind of inspiration at all. 'Verbal inspiration is the verbal form of the assault, but the attack is really aimed at inspiration itself.' He had no 'theory' of inspiration but a full persuasion of the fact. Clear communication, as Spurgeon well knew from his decades of trial, called for a right use of vocabulary, the proper construction of sentences, and the coherent arrangement of paragraphs. Aptness in illustration and example also was elemental to proper instruction. Verbal inspiration is far from a mere theory, therefore, but is a description of what actually

---

33. MTP 26:1566: 'Cheer for the Worker and Hope for London.' www.spurgeongems. org

took place. Nothing else would do for meaningful communication of truth from God's mind into words that will be open to human examination so 'that we might understand the things freely given to us of God' (1 Cor. 2:12).[34]

Since it is inspired, the Bible can be no other in matter of its content than infallible. Spurgeon asked, 'If this book be not infallible, where shall we find infallibility?' For good reason, Protestants have 'given up the Pope, for he has blundered often and terribly.' Shall we now substitute 'a horde of little popelings fresh from college. Are these correctors of Scripture infallible?' Is it certain that our Bibles are not right, but that the critics must be so?[35] Spurgeon did not look for confirmation of Scripture from philosophers or scientists as warrant for believing it. We would not see its authority 'as a grant from the enemies of God'. They can add nothing to its truthfulness or its power, for it is 'the sword of the Spirit'. Spurgeon did not suspend his confidence in Scripture on consent from external confirmation – 'because the philosophic mind consents to our doing so' – but in its self-authenticating authority. 'If scientists agree to our believing a part of the Bible, we thank them for nothing: we believe it whether or no.' Sooner would a Frenchman lay legitimate claim to London than a scientist lay claim to authority over the Bible. 'God being with us we shall not cease from this glorying,' the dying preacher reaffirmed, 'but will hold the whole of revealed truth, even to the end.'[36]

---

34. *The Greatest Fight in the World*, p. 67.
35. Ibid., p. 68.
36. Ibid., pp. 78, 79.

11

A SUMMARY OF
The Child is Father of the Man

Charles Spurgeon exemplified the biblical principle that 'He who loves wisdom makes his father glad' (Prov. 29:3). Spurgeon's many years of wise living characterized by faithfulness to biblical truth made his father glad, his grandfather glad, and honored the grace given him by his heavenly Father. This book has isolated ten issues that appeared early in Spurgeon's life, made their way in his ministry through the years, and stayed with him until death.

We have seen that Spurgeon recognized God's providence as a strong matter of biblical teaching and that he learned to interpret his life as an outworking of God's good pleasure toward him. From childhood in Stambourne, to the circumstances of his conversion, to his first sermon, to his first pastorate at Waterbeach, to his call to London, Spurgeon traced gratefully the marks of providence in his life. Even the times of trial and ridicule were gifts from God's decree to remind him of the undiluted graciousness of God's dealing with His people.

We have seen that Spurgeon's acquaintance with the doctrines of grace began early. His grandfather's library, the preaching of his father and grandfather, and his personal reading of Scripture convinced him of the reality of the eternal covenant of redemption.

He called these doctrines the 'staff of my manhood and the glory of my old age'. They filled his heart with assurance and filled his sermons with unction. He loved to sound the 'jubilee note of the trumpet of free grace'. Luke's picture of the repenting publican needs to be placed in the 'national portrait gallery of men saved by sovereign grace'. None were saved but those saved by sovereign grace. 'Could your tears forever flow, could your grief no respite know, you would have no claim upon the sovereign grace of God, who will have mercy on whom He will have mercy.'[1] Because of these doctrines, Spurgeon could with true hope hold forth mercy to his hearers and believe in God's propitious stance toward sinners. With all his heart he knew that by the foolishness of what he preached God saved sinners. Even as they had saving power, so they upheld him through controversy and in the time of death.

Sired, grand-sired and reared within pedobaptist independency, Spurgeon decided before conversion that the immersion of believers was the only true baptism. He was driven to this by a challenge from an Anglican teacher. Their discussion made him decide that he was unbaptized and that if ever divine grace should work a change in him, he would be baptized as a believer by immersion. His public baptism in a river washed away his shyness to be food for the fish. During his ministry, he baptized thousands in like manner. His church was one of the most historically esteemed and prominent churches in the Baptist Union. When he resigned from the Baptist Union over doctrinal issues, he assured friends that he had not ceased to be a Baptist.

Spurgeon stood in awe of preaching from his earliest memories of observing the earnestness of both preparation and delivery in his father and grandfather. Within three months of his conversion, he wrote his mother expressing his hope that one day she would rejoice to see him, 'the unworthy instrument of God, preaching to others.' Spurgeon loved the revealed Word as written in the Bible, for it

---

1. SEE 4:184, 187, 188.

awakened him; but he looked with particular awe at the preached Word, for it saved him. Even before he preached his first sermon, he imagined that one day he would preach sermons which would be printed. His dream came true to the number of over 3,500 sermons. He loved preaching. He studied and promoted it as both an art and a science, but mainly as an overflow of passion for divine truth as centered on the person and work of Christ. 'I am afraid I do not convey to you the pleasure of my own soul,' he told his congregation in considering how Jesus' blood cleanses from all sin, 'in turning over this thought, but it has charmed me beyond measure.'[2] As he compared modernist preachers to real gospel preachers, he observed that in the demeanor of the latter he could discern a true love for what they did. The pulpit was a throne, not a dreaded irrelevancy. It was a bridge between eternal life and endless death, not a rostrum for meaningless speculation. He looked at them and could see their very eyes sparkle and their souls glow, while enlarging upon free grace and dying love. So it was with him.

Also, we have observed that Spurgeon believed that everything done by the Church must have an evangelistic intent. His first impulse after conversion was to seek the conversion of his siblings. The Church exists for the glory of God, and God has invested His glory in the saving of sinners through the work of His beloved Son. Every benevolence sought souls; every sermon pled with sinners; every book pointed to the saving work of Christ; every church member should discover their gift and put it to use for the salvation of sinners. He defended D. L. Moody, supported evangelists from his Pastors' College, held special evangelistic meetings while issuing cautions against evangelistic contrivances that sought superficial and quick decisions. Though he saw a continuous stream of conversions week after week and heard of many conversions through his printed sermons, he still looked for a mighty flood of converting power to be poured out on the church.

---

2. MTP 16:231.

Though exuberant in his love of Christ, his love of the gospel, his love of the Church, and his love of preaching, Spurgeon had to deal with a physical constitution given to sickness and pain and a mental frame on the edge of depression. He told his congregation what was true of himself when he observed: 'Quite involuntarily, unhappiness of mind, depression of spirit, and sorrow of heart will come upon you. You may be without any real reason for grief, and yet may be among the most unhappy of men, because, for the time, your body has conquered your soul.' He confessed it early in his Christian pilgrimage, but also resolved that such debilities would not interrupt his determination to serve Christ with all his might. These personal tendencies were exacerbated by the public criticism that came his way from his first year in London even to the end of his life. The cruelty of caricatures, the falsehood contained in the press, and the Surrey Music Hall disaster of 1856 had a depressing influence on his spirit. Physical ailments sometimes received temporary relief through his yearly visit to the continent, most often to Mentone on the southern coast of France. Eventually, however, his body could not sustain the combination of gout, nephritis, and mental strain. Suffering produced a refined joy, provided necessary chastening, and transformed death into a friend. In 1887, Spurgeon told his people: 'Spiritual darkness of any sort is to be avoided, and not desired; and yet, surprising as it may seem to be, it is a fact that some of the best of God's people frequently walk in darkness; ay, some of them are wrapt in a sevenfold gloom at times, and to them neither sun, nor moon, nor stars appear.'[3] He knew that in Christ he found a fellow-sufferer of more deep physical suffering and more poignant troubles of soul. Spurgeon as a fallen sinner should expect such to be his lot, yet Christ was sinless and underwent it all for our sake.

We have seen also that Spurgeon thought of himself as something of a human paradigm. In his early letters he consistently referred to himself and his experiences and gave advice on the basis of what he

---

3. SS 19:351, 352.

was experiencing through God's dealing with his soul. He used his personal experience as a measure of the experience of all. He read books so others would not have to read them. He expected conviction of sin, struggles against that conviction, and eventual conversion to fit within the pattern of his personal experience. The way in which God humbles his ministers, the way in which one finds his way through intellectual difficulties, and the experimental verification of biblical truth – all these were elements of his experience that he might be a shepherd to others. Even in eternity, he postulated, the saving and sanctifying experience of the Christian minister will continue to serve as a lesson to the principalities and powers of the angelic world.

Spurgeon had not been a Christian long when he knew that he must be prepared for controversy. Within the first six months of conversion he reported, 'My enemies are many, and they hate me with cruel hatred.' This controversy came because he was a Calvinist and most of his fellows were 'Arminian' as he described them. Spurgeon knew that truth, in a fallen world in love with falsehood, always would be bound and hooded while being led to the scaffold. It was his duty consistently to present a defense for its innocence and seek its release. He challenged the falsehoods of the Church of England, of Roman Catholicism, of Latitudinarianism, of misleading literature, of moral and social evil, and of modernism. Controversy was never comforting but was an undeniable part of faithful stewardship of the gospel. The physical and mental strain of his last controversy, the Downgrade controversy, worked in combination with his advancing physical difficulties to bring him to death in the fifty-eighth year of his life.

In spite of the pain and sorrow of slander and opposition and the well-documented depressing effects it had on Spurgeon, he looked upon it all as a means of grace. Very early in his Christian walk, he was convinced of a 'sense of my own weakness, nothingness, and utter inability to do anything in and of myself, – I pray God that I may never lose it.' God would see to it that he did not. Except for the lies, Spurgeon accepted all the public hooting about his lack of education, his lack of sophistication, the confident air he manifested in the pulpit, and his throw-back theology as a means to make him have a candid view of himself and to give all the glory to God for obvious blessing on his ministry. He was nothing, he would admit; so, therefore, the gospel must be everything and must be doing all the work. When Spurgeon was demeaned, God's work was glorified. When the harlots, and the drunkards, and the back-alley scum came to hear him and were converted, he delighted in the reports of how unsophisticated his auditory was. Spurgeon looked to Scripture, found that God was slandered, Christ was slandered, Paul was slandered, and that, indeed, the Bible has a theology of slander. It is better to be abused and ridiculed than false to the Lord. He felt right at home with the world's anger at him, counted it his glory, and believed in a future vindication.

Undergirding all that Spurgeon preached, every ministry he initiated, every book he wrote, and every controversy in which he engaged was an unshaken faith in the infallibility of Scripture. In the month that he was converted, Spurgeon wrote his father, 'How beautiful is the Bible! I never loved it so before; it seems to me as necessary food.' That conviction never parted from Spurgeon. In 1891, at the last Pastors' College Conference, he preached:

> In proportion as your mind becomes saturated with Holy Scripture, you are conscious of being lifted right up, and carried aloft as on eagles' wings. You seldom come down from a solitary Bible reading without feeling that you have drawn near to God. ... If you keep close to the inspired book, you can suffer no harm; say rather you are at the fountain-head of all moral and spiritual good. This is food fit for men of God: this is the bread which nourishes the highest life.[4]

> Stern Lawgiver! yet thou dost wear
> The Godhead's most benignant grace;
> Nor know we anything so fair
> As is the smile upon thy face: (WORDSWORTH, *Ode To Duty*).

---

4. *The Greatest Fight in the World*, pp. 55, 57.

Those who die daily will die easily.... The man who rejoices in the covenant of grace is cheered by the fact that even death itself is comprehended among the things which belong to the believer. I would to God we had learned this lesson. We should not then put death aside amongst the lumber, nor set it upon the shelf among the things which we never intend to use. Let us live as dying men among dying men, and then we shall truly live. This will not make us unhappy; for surely no heir of heaven will fret because he is not doomed to live here forever. It were a sad sentence if we were bound over to dwell in this poor world forever. ... To grow ripe and to be carried home like shocks of corn in their season, is not this a fit and fair thing? To labour through a blessed day, and then at nightfall to go home and to receive the wages of grace – is there anything dark and dismal about that? ... If you are the Lord's own child, I invite you to look this home-going in the face until you ... see no more in it of gloom and dread, but a very heaven of hope.

CHARLES HADDON SPURGEON

BOOKS ABOUT SPURGEON REFERRED
TO BY THE AUTHOR

J. C. Carlile, *C. H. Spurgeon: An Interpretative Biography* (London: The Religious Tract Society, 1933).

Zack Eswine, *Spurgeon's Sorrows* (Ross-shire, Scotland: Christian Focus Publications, 2015).

Justin D. Fulton, *Charles H. Spurgeon, Our Ally* (Chicago, Philadelphia: H. J. Smith & Co., 1892).

Ernest LeVos, *C. H. Spurgeon and the Metropolitan Tabernacle: Addresses and Testimonials, 1854-1879* (Bloomington, IN: I Universe, 2014).

Iain H. Murray, *The Forgotten Spurgeon* (Edinburgh: The Banner of Truth Trust, 1966).

Iain H. Murray, *The Letters of Charles Haddon Spurgeon* (Edinburgh: The Banner of Truth Trust, 1992).

Henry Davenport Northrop, *Life and Works of Spurgeon* (Chicago, Philadelphia, Stockton, CA: Monarch Book Company, 1890).

G. Holden Pike, *The Life and Work of Charles Haddon Spurgeon*, 6 vols. (London: Cassel, 1898).

Charles Spurgeon, *The Letters of C. H. Spurgeon* (1923). He was the son of C. H. Spurgeon. http://www.romans45.org/spurgeon/misc/letters.htm.

Hannah Wyncoll, ed. *Wonders of Grace: Original Testimonies of Converts during Spurgeon's Early Years* (London: The Wakeman Trust, 2016).

BOOKS AND WRITINGS BY SPURGEON
REFERRED TO BY THE AUTHOR

A Good Start (Morgan, PA: Soli Deo Gloria Publications, 1995).

An All Round Ministry (Edinburgh: The Banner of Truth Trust, 1978).

Autobiography, 4 vols. (Chicago, New York, Toronto: Fleming H. Revell, 1894).

Christ's Glorious Achievements (Ross-shire, Scotland: Christian Focus Publications, 2019).

Commentary on Matthew (Springfield, MO: Particular Baptist Press, 2015).

Commenting and Commentaries (1876, rpt. Edinburgh: The Banner of Truth Trust, 1969).

The Greatest Fight in the World (Ross-shire, Scotland: Christian Focus Publications, 2014).

The King's Highway (Ross-shire, Scotland: Christian Focus Publications, 1989).

The Saint and His Saviour (Ross-shire, Scotland: Christian Focus Publications, 2009).

The Sword and Trowel. Monthly magazine published by Spurgeon between 1865 and 1889.

The Treasury of David (Old Time Gospel Hour).

COLLECTIONS OF SERMONS REFERRED TO BY THE AUTHOR

A Treasury of Spurgeon on the Life and Work of our Lord, 6 vols (Grand Rapids: Baker Book House, 1979).

New Park Street Pulpit (referred to as NPSP, with volume number and sermon number).

Metropolitan Tabernacle Pulpit (referred to as MTP, with volume number and sermon number).

Sermons of Rev. C. H. Spurgeon, 20 volumes (New York: Funk & Wagnalls, 1857–1892). This series contains some sermons that were not published in the *New Park Street Pulpit* and the *Metropolitan Tabernacle Pulpit.* It will be referred to as SS, along with the volume number and page number.

Spurgeon's Expository Encyclopedia, 15 vols (Grand Rapids: Baker Book House, 1977).

Christian George, Ed. *The Lost Sermons of C. H. Spurgeon: His Earliest Outlines and Sermons Between 1851 and 1854* (Nashville: B&H, 2016).

Index

Also available from Christian Focus Publications...

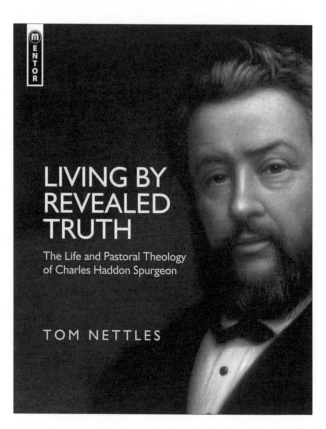

LIVING BY
REVEALED
TRUTH

The Life and Pastoral Theology
of Charles Haddon Spurgeon

TOM NETTLES

Living by Revealed Truth

The Life and Pastoral Theology of Charles Haddon Spurgeon

Tom J. Nettles

Tom Nettles has spent more than 15 years working on this magisterial biography of Charles Haddon Spurgeon, the famous 19th century preacher and writer. More than merely a biography it covers his life, ministry and also provides an indepth survey of his theology.

... takes us into the heart of Charles Spurgeon's conviction and his pastoral theology. This is a book that will encourage, educate, and bless its readers.

R. Albert Mohler
President, The Southern Baptist Theological Seminary, Louisville, Kentucky

Charles Haddon Spurgeon was the greatest preacher of the nineteenth century in England and probably the whole world. The pungent and passionate sermons of the Baptist pastor brought home the gospel message to the hearts of his numerous hearers and more numerous readers. Tom Nettles has retold Spurgeon's life as a warm admirer, but he is careful to rest his judgements on detailed evidence. In particular The Sword and the Trowel, the magazine Spurgeon edited as pastor of the Metropolitan Tabernacle in London, is used as a quarry for an abundance of fresh material. Consequently this biography casts new light on Spurgeon's life, ministry and theology.

David Bebbington
Professor of History, University of Stirling, Stirling

ISBN 978-1-7819-1122-8

ZACK ESWINE

"...an incredibly practical guide"
SCOTTY WARD SMITH

SPURGEON'S
SORROWS

Realistic Hope for those
who Suffer from Depression

Spurgeon's Sorrows

Realistic Hope for those who Suffer from Depression

Zack Eswine

Christians should have the answers, shouldn't they? Depression affects many people both personally and through the ones we love. Here Zack Eswine draws from C.H Spurgeon, 'the Prince of Preachers' experience to encourage us. What Spurgeon found in his darkness can serve as a light in our own darkness. Zack Eswine brings you here, not a self–help guide, rather 'a handwritten note of one who wishes you well.'

In an age of quick answers Spurgeon speaks beyond the grave with heart-felt understanding and solace. Those who know the pain of such suffering find in these pages a level of succour for the soul which both normalizes and gives hope...a rare insight into the experience of a ubiquitous problem.

Margaret Reynolds
Counselor and Co-Founder of Grace Counselling & Conciliation Services, Auckland, New Zealand

Eswine's work demonstrates the value of reading biographies, old books, and sermons. Interacting with godly men and women from church history can be a vital aid to Christian maturity. He handles Spurgeon carefully, yet provocatively at points, and produces a volume that promises to help pastors and laypeople confront the sad terror of the dark night of the soul.

The Gospel Coalition

ISBN 978-1-7819-1538-7

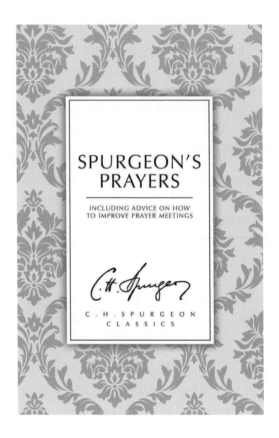

SPURGEON'S PRAYERS

INCLUDING ADVICE ON HOW
TO IMPROVE PRAYER MEETINGS

C . H . S P U R G E O N
C L A S S I C S

Spurgeon's Prayers

C. H. SPURGEON

Listening to someone else pray gives you an insight into their mind - their hopes, concerns, and understanding of their relationship with God. Spurgeon thought that prayer was a measure of the vitality of the church - he once ushered some visitors into the prayer meeting at his church with the words 'would you like to see the church's power plant?' These are Spurgeon's prayers taken down as he prayed them. You can learn a lot about how to pray by studying their structure and content. Each short prayer shows you the knowledge of the Bible he had and his understanding of human needs.

ISBN 978-1-5271-0118-0

AROUND
the
WICKET
GATE

Help for Those Who Only
Know *About* Christ

C. H. SPURGEON

Around the Wicket Gate

Help For Those Who Only Know *About* Christ

C. H. Spurgeon

The greatest of all tragedies must be that of the person who dies just outside the gate of life. They are standing, as it were, just outside the wicket gate to the church grounds – seeing the beauty of the building, knowing the people going in – but not stepping over the threshold themselves. Almost saved but altogether lost.

This is a book of immeasurable value to those who have some knowledge of the Christian Faith but who are resisting God's call to commit their lives to him. No Christian should be without a copy, to either lend or give away to a friend or acquaintance who may be lingering at the gate.

Around the Wicket Gate is written in Spurgeon's unique style – sharp, penetrating, and easily readable. One of the most quoted preachers of modern times, his sermons have proved to be a blessing to millions. For someone thinking about Christianity, who has yet to accept Christ as their saviour, reading this book could help them towards the most important step they ever take.

… one of the most famous books that the kind, loving, extraordinary Christian, C. H. Spurgeon, ever wrote. If you are just mildly interested in what is a Christian and how people become followers of Jesus Christ, then there is no more straightforward and fascinating book for you to read but this.

Geoff Thomas
Conference Speaker and author, Aberystwyth, Wales

ISBN 978-1-5271-0341-2

Christian Focus Publications

Our mission statement –

STAYING FAITHFUL

In dependence upon God we seek to impact the world through literature faithful to His infallible Word, the Bible. Our aim is to ensure that the Lord Jesus Christ is presented as the only hope to obtain forgiveness of sin, live a useful life and look forward to heaven with Him.

Our books are published in four imprints:

CHRISTIAN FOCUS

Popular works including biographies, commentaries, basic doctrine and Christian living.

CHRISTIAN HERITAGE

Books representing some of the best material from the rich heritage of the church.

MENTOR

Books written at a level suitable for Bible College and seminary students, pastors, and other serious readers. The imprint includes commentaries, doctrinal studies, examination of current issues and church history.

CF4•K

Children's books for quality Bible teaching and for all age groups: Sunday school curriculum, puzzle and activity books; personal and family devotional titles, biographies and inspirational stories – because you are never too young to know Jesus!

Christian Focus Publications Ltd,
Geanies House, Fearn, Ross-shire,
IV20 1TW, Scotland, United Kingdom.
www.christianfocus.com